Mirror Mirror

Restoring the Distorted Self Image

WANDA I PEREZ

A H Fleming, Author
CMC

Mirror Mirror
Wanda I Perez
by A H Fleming

Printed in the United States of America

ISBN 978-0-9847322-7-2

Hidden Potential Series
Published by
Creative Media Concepts

CONTENTS

INTRODUCTION

I t is said that a picture is worth a 1,000 words; our lives are image driven; the proliferation of media in this information age bombards our lives with images from around the world. These images can create a great sense of well being and allow us to share memorable moments with loved ones or persons we only know through images and our perceptions. Images shape how we feel and can help shape our perspective of ourselves, others, and the world around us. Instantaneous images certainly have made the world a much smaller place.

Not all imagery is positive. If you watch the news you can feel hopeless and disconnected. Image after image of crime, death, terrorism, political points of view, and countless stories of doom can change your outlook from optimistic to pessimistic very quickly.

It seems recently most entertainment has become reality TV and its depictions mostly of scandal and mayhem. TV producers now more than ever have an effect on the public psyche as well as dialogue more than ever. It's not just TV; the proliferation of the internet has made privacy a thing of the past. Almost instantly you can see a child involved in a hit and run in China, murder of an outgoing political figure and a dog in Tennessee who befriended an elephant killed and have more compassion showed for him than we show toward each other.

Healing is necessary in our world today like never before. We are damaged from the distortions made of images of ourselves and others in this world that seeks to define all of us and move us into polarizing camps. Politics now does not accept moderation but growing dissidents into separate camps growing wider by rhetoric and shrill voices who speak for the invisible masses.

Our values are under assault by images of people who have no real talent and add no value to the expression of our humanity past the latest sex tape and designer dress. We need to heal and become healthy families and individuals of contribution, production and substance.

The first step to true healing is to be able to unplug from negative images for a period of time and become more self aware and replace the negative with positive images. Self awareness is being able to connect to who you are without the programming of the culture, family and others. Achieving goals or becoming someone different is easiest accomplished by setting goals, learning how to create images of them, focus and take action toward achieving them.

Who are you really, how do you feel and what is important to you. This time can be used for true inspiration by becoming more introspective and asking the tough questions about your feelings, emotional state, relationships, and the actions that have lead to the outcomes you have experienced in your life.

What happens when the person you feel strongly about or hate is not an image on the TV or in a magazine? They are not half way across the world swearing allegiance to another flag, eating different food and speaking a different language. What happens when the person you can't stand is you? I could not begin to tell you how many people I have met that literally hate the person they are and would love to be anyone else but themselves.

I realized that much of my life I was misunderstood and underappreciated. Not just by my family, friends, and co-workers but by myself. When I have accepted the challenges of life and started dedicating myself to learning and becoming more aware of what I was capable of, I discovered that I was stronger and smarter than I ever thought I was. I learned through hard times that I could budget my money, learn new secrets to wealth and prosper in my career and relationships.

This book is partly my story, more importantly it's our story. The story of a young child misunderstood, molested, betrayed and never finding any type of love of myself until I was almost a golden girl. Yes, this is our story; dreams of little girls with pig tails and dolls who have come to deeply despise they way they look and feel about themselves. Turning what seemed larger than life moments into baggage or better yet cargo that is stored for a life time until it can fit no more and the anger and self hatred begin to spill out.

There has been much to say about self esteem, both low esteem and its effects and how to become a person of high self esteem. I think the way you feel about yourself can not be underestimated. I journeyed a long way to write this book and I suspect that you did as well in reading it. If you are wiling to go a little further maybe together we can develop a healthy self image and learn to enjoy this ride together without the self mutilating thoughts and emotions that haunt us everyday.

It is empowering to feel good about ourselves and our lives but most people have trouble transitioning this feeling of low esteem to one of high esteem. These negative feelings about ourselves and the world around us can destroy and negate the possibilities in front of us. I remember a time that there was not much in front of me. Just more of the same, empty expectations and unfulfilled desires as a woman, a person, someone lost and without hope for the future.

I believe the reason for this and why the dreams for many people has not worked is because feelings are hard to interpret and not easy to change. Self concept that comes originally out of our experiences can eventually develop into images that we live up or down to. My experiences taught me plenty but the lessons that I learned did not make me whole but kept open the hole in my chest that later filled my body with cancer and tumors that were only a manifestation of the disease that had always eaten away at me.

The challenges of my life and learning to live through cancer taught me to fight. There were long days of despair and even times that I literally told myself to give up. Close friends along with something inside myself, something that I had not known before about myself would not let me let go. I had cancer of the esophagus, stomach, and thyroid. I also had tumors in my breasts and ovaries. Today I am cancer free but what many people don't know is that I can not eat fiber; just small meals of mostly chicken, pasta, and potatoes. I hope to share more of my story with you later.

For many women the person in the mirror is not the image of beauty but imperfection and for many someone much worse. It was a friend who reminded me of my reflection. He reminded me that my truest reflection many times is only seen in the ones we love and influence in our lives. They are our truest reflection and at best hope for the future; our legend.

Self concept which is what you think about yourself manifests itself in life images that are many times distortions of who we really are because they are partly defined by experiences and reinforced by negative imagery of society, ourselves, and people close to us.

Distorted images of self can go beyond self esteem and literally distort a once promising life because we project these distorted images into every relationship and opportunity. The way we think about our selves is our self concept, our feelings about ourselves is how we esteem of value ourselves, but imagery is the powerful image of ourselves that is crystallized feelings and thoughts. Images are powerful representations internally expressed through images.

Symbols and imagery are even more powerful than feelings because they are like looped tapes that play over and over becoming our reference point to who we are and yes, how we feel and think about our self and our lives. This book will allow you to identify the people and things that shaped your image of you and allow you to become the voice in your life that reshapes and moves your life down a path of your own choosing. Life begins with a new image of your self.

I am fortunate to be writing this book under the Living the Max Life umbrella of resources to assist people in defining and navigating their lives. We are developing a system that is called Hidden Potential. My mission is to work with women just like you and I who have struggled with issues of life to create our own professional and personal expression in the world to find healing, purpose, and realized potential.

Ayub Fleming, Author

I have been fortunate in being able to work with people like Wanda Perez. Wanda has become a dear friend and it has been my privilege to help write and publish this book for her.

I wanted to share a little of our story and history as we have walked together. Below you will find an excerpt from Reflections and free e-book provided by *Living the Max Life*. I hope that as you read these pages that something inside you comes alive and create a new hope for a new image and life.

Peace be with you on your journey of excellence and new personal expression.

The following is an excerpt from an e-book called **Reflections**.

Reflections was inspired when I was sitting in (Starbucks) with a very special friend and colleague who I shared of lot of my life with. One thing I am grateful for is that we have shared the beauty and splendor of life. It's one of those rare relationships where the most important thing we established up front was to allow the other person to be totally honest and to not judge the expression of the other. We learned just to throw it out there and let the other person react. At times it has caused us great liberation and at times, great pain.

To complicate things we are of a different language, nationality and culture. We have had to work on not just taking things at face value but making sure that we under-stand each other and what we are trying to communicate before reacting. Trust me, we have had plenty of arguments until we began to learn that our position or need to be right is not as important as our need to connect and be understood. Overtime we have learned that the language of acceptance and intimacy of emotion is a universal language. Something that all mankind needs to learn.

In one conversation though I remember the thought she had of her own life and mortality. I remember her speaking only of her failures in tones of doubt that in my view did not describe her at all. In that moment I thought about her impact on my life and the life of many others. If I were to describe her would I use the same words and tone that she did. The answer was no.

I would later reflect as I saw this person in all her frailty speak to individuals and crowds teaching them to overcome fear and live life to its fullest. In speaking to others how many of her own fears she has had to overcome in the process. Maybe in filtering out our fears through focusing on someone else we find the strength to make a difference in their lives as well as our own.

One evening, I was sitting across from my friend and remember seeing her reflection in the glass and I thought about how much I saw her reflection in me as well as her children and in all the lives she is changing. In her reflection I saw a person full of compassion and love. Many times at level of caring and giving of her self that I never found me capable of, at least not from my perspective or my view of how I see myself. I saw physically a person maturing in age and changes that come with time yet an obvious beauty and underlying image of greatness that shown from the inside out.

She would go on to form a Foundation with her promise to "Transition lives with love". Her foundation focuses *on assisting abused and homeless women and children. In her previous work as homeownership counseling I saw her change one life at a time by giving hope and opportunity to people that would have never experienced unless someone like Wanda reached out to the; not just giving knowledge about the process, procedures, and subsides but about responsibility and sharing the principles of success in life with unparalleled compassion and transparency. To reach the vulnerable and weak sometimes you must become both in order to move them from familiar states to more empowering states that make their dreams possible.*

I wonder sometimes what it would like be like if our description of ourselves was an accurate reflection of our accomplishments, failures, our relationships, and our legacy that we begrudgingly leave behind. My hope is that you will have someone in your life see you with some accuracy and help paint a truer picture of yourself. You may find it in your children, the one you love, and hopefully in our dreams yet to be fulfilled.

In this expression of triumph, hope, and love take some time and reflect on your life as it is, as it could be, and what you are willing to do to make your life meaningful. Remember, in your journey you are never alone. In the mirror of life we always see more than one reflection. Remember no road leads to nowhere. Each road is paved with a destination in mind. Let it be the destination that you choose for yourself.

Reflections Journal, Written by: Ayub Fleming

Chapter 1

Mirror Mirror

If you allow me to define you, I can manipulate you into what I want you and need you to be not for yourself but for me.

Ayub Fleming

How I see you matters only to you, how you see yourself matters to the world.

Ayub Fleming

Who is the fairest of them all? This subject is close to me because I like so many millions of people have suffered and rotted in a mental jail of my own creation. It was a jail that seemed real but was made of smoke and mirrors, mere shadows of the truth. I don't know how I got here but I remember when I was released. I vowed vengeance on my jailer, the judge, and jury. I realized that I was put in jail on trumped up charges and was convicted by my own hands. I was the judge, juror and my own executioner.

I look back and often wonder what the mirrors of my child hood were. I grew up a poor young girl in Canovanas, Puerto Rico with my fifteen family members made of my three sisters and 12 cousins in a small 3 bedroom house. They were happy times for the most part as I look back, but there were storms brewing over the horizon just out of sight for a young girl growing up poor in the country.

As I think back much of my life is imagery. When I feel pain in my life I often drift back into the mountains were I grew up and I remember my grandfather. How I wish he was here to hold me again as a child and tell me that it would be okay. In Puerto Rico the mountains are very beautiful and I remember the cool breeze and smell of the mountains.

I could go on and on but looking back it seemed that my life is made of images that either comfort me much like my grandfather or my dog boogie. My dog boogie would go with me into the mountains to feed the chickens or just spend quiet time with me. I remember long walks and conversations as he would look at me with his big eyes and tilt his head as I spoke as if he understood every word. He was a girl's best friend.

The images from times long gone can also be painful as I remember other less memorable things from my childhood. I was too young to suffer some of the things that young girls suffer, many of you know the pain of innocence lost to uncles and cousins, family members who were supposed to love and protect us. The images now are mirrors that I confront myself in as

I have to fight for my own definitions of what I am and what I am capable of. Mirrors at times must be cleaned to show forth the true beauty of the one looking into it; others were shattered and broken because they are deceitful. I scream to be free; I am not my past experiences though I am still challenged by them. In life we have many mirrors and images that are ingrained in our mind; mirrors that define us.

"I was too young to suffer some of the things that young girls suffer"

We will talk more about these images later but let me explain what I mean when I talk about mirrors. The image we have of ourselves is a crystallized version of our self concept and esteem or how we really feel about ourselves. Mirrors are the reflection within problems caused by these images. The mirrors are empowering or disempowering but they tell us plenty about what is going on inside of us.

When you are confronted by problems it is not just the present situation that is speaking to you. Your past is speaking to you. When we experience an incident of significant pain or pleasure in an event or relationship that begins to shape or shift how we think and feel. It does because of our need to avoid the pain of it or recreate the pleasure of the experience. It is natural to avoid pain and move toward the things in our life that bring us joy.

For me many times when I was confronted by a problem I chose different reactions but the result for me was hiding from what I really was. When confronted with problems many times I saw an image of someone who was always blamed, never loved and not capable of doing the simplest things.

My grandfather was the first mirror that reflected an image back to me. He was a kind man, short and stocky. I remember being his favorite; he would always make sure I had the best of everything. In these simple times I remember his comfort, most of which I would not understand until later that there is a price to pay for everything in life. To this day whenever I am stressed I look for my grandfather to comfort me, he reminds me most of the mountains. He is long gone now, but his reflection lives on in me, as mine will live on either for good or bad in my children and the people that I have touched with my life.

Our images are not all bad some of them are very good and empowering. They are powerful and when we think about ourselves, the people and circumstances that make up our lives its how we evaluate what they mean to us that determine our response and how we interact with them. Those thoughts and feelings are represented to us in images.

I wonder if I challenged you today to start living your life on your own terms and stop letting outside influences shape how you feel, how you see yourself and the possibilities of your life would you get up and walk or continue to lay there shifting ever so slightly to find a comfortable spot in the midst of your pain. I had to make tough choices in my life, including moving from Puerto Rico on my own with my young daughter and son. No money or job, I came to the United States to make a better living and move forward with my life.

I was wrapped up in fear and anger about my life and just about everyone in it. When everything told me that I could not, I dug deep down and found something true inside myself and found a way to say yes to a better future. How about you, what are you hiding from? Who have you allowed to tell you can't do this or that, that being a woman, black, brown, white, Asian, or Latino is less or is a stumbling block?

I know who am I to talk to you that way? I mean I don't even know you. "Nobody knows the trouble I've seen, nobody knows but Jesus!" I know cry me a river. I am talking to you that way because I have dedicated a large part of my life to understanding and improving the lives of others. One thing that I am convinced of is that individuals have a creative greatness within them and a right to express it. We don't know how to access it and what to do about it. I am writing this to you and if you are reading it then I think you are ready to change and define your life on your own terms.

"I dug deep down and found something true inside myself and found a way to say yes to a better future"

I know how you feel; I had plenty of pain and not much else. My grandfather who at the time I believed to be my father and grandmother was my mother. They were the only parents that I knew until I was eight years old. The relationship that I had with my grandfather who was my comforter and protector soon would be replaced by a father who was an abusive drunk for the next 10 years of my life.

Okay, you are successful in some areas of your life, but do really think that you are living up to your full potential? Are you satisfied at this point in your journey that all your unfinished business and the way you truly look in the mirror at yourself has no affect on the quality of your life? Trust me it does and we are going to talk about it and get clear on how you develop your self image, how it is distorted and how to repair the broken image inside you.

I started this chapter and called it mirror mirror because most of us use external experiences and things to define our self concept (what we think) that helps shape our self esteem (how we feel) and develop a self image (how we see ourselves). This self image if distorted shows you only a part or none of your authentic self.

Story   "Am I insecure"

The following story is told by Ayub Fleming.

I was sitting one evening at a restaurant having lunch with a friend. She was and is attractive with a nice personality and fully capable of doing far greater things that she has done in the past. Knowing her I know she can be moody and even angry at times. All the while masking her true image of herself and how she has begun to see her life. This distorted image is at conflict with who she really thinks that she is and shows in her personality and behavior.

In this conversation she asked me," am I insecure", I asked her what she meant by the question "do you think that I am insecure". She thought for a moment and as I could see smoke trickling from one ear, I thought I better stop her. Before I could she answered, "No, I am not insecure, but what do you think". I said if you think that you are not insecure what does it matter what I think.

The problem was two fold. She asked the question because she was insecure. If she was not then there would have been no reason to seek my validation of who she was. Second her ego would not allow her to be honest. Since she was on the path of lying to herself and for me to tell her otherwise would trigger uncertainty in her and possibly resentment; than my opinion did not matter.

Well you say, "What kind of friend are you". I would respond an honest one. She would have been better off asking herself the question, "What do I have to believe about myself in order to feel insecure". She could have better shaped her life not by asking others but by introspection and asking herself.

Once she could have begun to look at the experiences that have occurred and how they affected her beliefs she could have asked a more empowering question to start reshaping her thought process. Questions like "What could I believe about my self or this situation that could empower me to feel that I am secure in myself and my ability to affect my future".

The second question allows us to inventory of ourselves and seek the answers or resources for things that we lack. The experiences and how we evaluated them and how that shaped the way we think and feel. This open display of our lives allows for better examination of the facts and allows us to change them.

Self image is powerful. Don't underestimate its ability to shape your life. Starting looking for things internally as well as things close to you that affirm you rather than tear you down. Self image when taken to an extreme like body dismorphic disease which can be deadly. Can you not see the beautiful women or handsome man in the mirror, does being a little thin or overweight really make your life void of meaning or purpose. In image driven media and competitive society where image is worshipped it can make a child who feels that they don't measure up completely null and void.

"Who is the fairest of them all?"

"Who are you asking?"

There was another mirror that began to shape my life as one of the darkest periods of my life. This stage of my life was shaped by my father as well as other men in my life who molested me, abused me and offered no sense of self worth, value or protection.

In that reflection I saw a fading image of a little girl who was afraid and angry; never loved. What was worse is my real mother began to refer to me for years as her little boy. My father always wanted a son and it did not happen with my two older sisters so I was their last hope and it turned what seemed to be their deepest disappointment.

Even to this day I struggle with the concept of love and what it means. I never feel comfortable with it or in it. I think it is hard for most women; we don't seem to be first in anyone's life any more including our own. In most relationships we settle for what we have for reasons of security and loneliness and we don't develop ourselves and develop patience for something better. We end up mere objects for the pleasure of others with names like mother, sister, wife, or girlfriend, that sometime honestly are not fulfilling when we are not totally invested in them for us and not just by the labeling of others.

"In that reflection I saw a fading image of a little girl who was afraid and angry; never loved"

It is easy to loose our identity and just assume roles assigned to us by someone else. We readily accepting them as nurtures and care givers and are relegated to not even having a name other than your husbands wife. We also don't participate in setting up the rules in how things work. Somewhere that is decided for us; we are relegated to the children's table, cleaning and accepting roles of caregiver and part time lover.

There were many mirrors in my life that shaped my thoughts, image and eventually my behavior. I remember times of rage and anger where I seemingly had little control over what I said or did. I think at some points I did not even care. My life did not feel or resemble anything of who I felt that I was on the inside. I kept looking for mountains but only found more mirrors that reflected the same old image of this broken little girl.

What are the mirrors in your life? They are simply the experiences and circumstances that cause a reflection of you in them. In your past did you see yourself as weak, victimized, powerful, beautiful or intelligent? Mirrors have a way of reflecting back our evaluation of what we experience and how we see ourselves.

As we grow older we have an opportunity to go back and not take the blame for things that we did not do and accept responsibility for the things that we did. To see ourselves differently than what the negative life lessons taught us. To empower ourselves to finally be worthy of a good life, self love and to forgive those who have hurt us.

Image Coaching:

Accept the fact that you have an image about your-self that is either empowering or negative and you are living up or down to it. At the very least it is distorted and holding you back from what you could be as well as accomplish.

Start writing in your journal about how you think, feel, and how you see yourself emotionally and physi-cally. Notice how you feel and react under pressure; take the time to describe how you feel, what you are saying to yourself and what you do physically during this experience.

When you feel bad or are very emotional ask yourself questions that make you examine yourself.

Put empowering questions in play to understand what you think, how you feel, and what you see.

Begin to write and practice affirmations of who you really are and who you want to be.

Along with affirmations practice the daily habit of coaching yourself. Self talk is powerful and happens whether you direct it or not. Take an active role by coaching yourself daily.

Before I go on, I wanted to share a little story with you on how I got started in homeownership counseling, writing books, and doing other things to try and help people achieve their dreams. I think it all started about 15 years ago when I moved from Puerto Rico on my own. I was a college graduate with a degree in communications and had two small children.

I had a disappointing marriage in which my thoughts and feelings again did not matter. Promises made were promises un-kept and I got to a point like many that I could not take it anymore. I found myself in a new country and not being able to speak or write English very well.

What I did have was a fierce determination to make it, though I struggled with low esteem and fear of many things. I think some people who know me would describe me as stubborn. I think that this is true but in some areas it has served me well. At the time that I moved I had to go on public assistance for a while but I was determined to make it. It was not going to be the condition that I settled for.

Through a series of events and God placing people in my path to help me I landed good jobs, I worked hard and I made real progress in my life. One job in particular, I became the senior housing counselor for a local housing authority. I was able to be a part of something special as I was able to assist people in becoming homeowners who were previously homeless, current section 8 participants, and person who would have never been able to obtain homeownership without some government programs and a lot of help.

Many people were in the program for more than 4 years and were dedicated themselves to reaching their dreams. If they bought into the program and were dedicated, there was no way I was going to let them down.

My first development was Hampton Park a beautiful community in the heart of Central Florida. We had several homes on site and several off site that we could assist people into getting into homes. There were so many hearts that were changed and people began to not only believe in the impossible but began to walk in it. We met meeting after meeting and in some cases year after year but both them and I achieved our goals and were forever changed by the experience. I still see many of my old clients today and almost all of them had maintained their homes in good standing against the odds. You can believe and achieve the impossible.

Some time later as I was meeting with a former co-worker and friend; he encouraged me to start a foundation. I was already working with families and different charity type events with the Catholic Church and other organizations but needed something that was more organized and now was my vision for helping others. At the time he suggested the unthinkable, not only to start my own foundation but to use my name as the name for the foundation. After much deliberation and struggle the WP Foundation Inc., was born in 2005.

Imagine that a poor farm girl from Canovanas Puerto Rico from humble beginnings sleeping several to a room on the floor to running nationally recognized homeownership programs and starting her own foundation.

In 2004 I was touched by a family; they were a husband and wife with 2 little boys. The two little boys were very close in age. At the time this was the second year that I had been sponsoring families from the Orlando Coalition for the Homeless for Christmas. This year I learned that it is truly more blessed to give than receive.

I had gotten their ages from their counselor and their wish list for Christmas. They had asked for a few clothes and some toys for the kids. I remember it was a cold day when we met close to Christmas. I had completed the shopping and loaded up my family to go and meet them at the shelter. We met in a small outdoor playground area where the families congregated during the day. We all introduced our selves and started in polite conversation. I told them that my family and I were happy to share Christmas with them.

When I gave the mother of the two boys a jacket she broke down and cried. I asked her why she was crying and she told me that she had never had a new jacket in her life. The two boys gasped and almost exploded with every toy that was opened. We spent a lot of time with them that day playing and laughing.

The next morning I decided to do something extra for them, there was just something about those kids that I needed to touch and be touched by. I took them with a friend to McDonalds and we bought them breakfast. I remember walking up to the counter and them looking puzzled asking if they could order what they wanted, "anything you want" we shot back. We enjoyed breakfast with them but we had another surprise. We bought some disposable cameras and gave them to them and drove them out to Disney World for the day. No rules just have fun for a day.

I am grateful that we were able to provide a nice holiday for them. More toys and Christmas cheer for my family would have been the norm but it was time to share more than just a nod and silent prayer passing people on the street it was time to bump into a few and get to know them.

Some time had passed and we had not seen the family again for some time. We saw the two little boys coming out of the woods one day waving to us as we passed by and on another occasion catching the bus while I was sitting down having a cup of coffee. It seems that we touched them in a lasting way before they disappeared back into their lives. I have not seen them for years but in my day dreams I see them as young men waving to me and letting me know that they are okay.

I pray for them having learned that their mother had been arrested and the family struggling to make it. As I looked at my son with so many choices I could not help but wonder about those two little boys. What images now stare back at them in the mirrors of their chaotic lives?

We pressed on and through that time we have sponsored hundreds of families in Central Florida through our Christmas Wish program and in Dominican Republic both for Christmas and our back to school drives.

I could not be more grateful for the help of each and every sponsor as well as each and every family that allows us to touch them. I will be sharing more stories about the Christmas Wish as well as the foundation later.

Chapter 2

7 Years of Bad Luck

To live in prison is to live without mirrors. To live without mirrors is to live without the self.
Atwood, Margaret Eleanor

A reflection of life is not life
Jonathan Huie

I used the chapter title as a metaphor because there is an old saying that if you break a mirror, you get 7 years of bad luck. I have literally known people who lived much of their lives not looking into mirrors not because of some superstition because it was easier not to look at themselves. The pain and isolation of looking at someone everyday who does not look like what you represent to yourself or the world on the inside is too painful.

I remember for years not really looking at the person in the mirror. I never liked what I saw. I was a girl but my mom kept calling me her little boy. I had to fight like one and swallow the pain of the beatings like one to survive. Though I always thought of myself as a girl, her labeling me confused me and made me adopt many masculine traits; traits that would haunt me and do much damage to the relationships in my life.

My father in our home had a way of angling all the mirrors in the house so he could always see himself as well as keep an eye on us. He controlled the images for those 10 years until I had no image of my own that was not dictated by him. I never realized until much later in life where I was confronted by something other than pain and control, it was love that shattered the broken image but the affects of those distorted images lasted much longer.

Breaking away from some of the external things that define us won't bring 7 years of bad luck. It will bring the beginning of a new life, one where you are empowered and can appreciate the creation that the world has been waiting for.

No don't look around, I am not talking to the person behind you, I am talking directly to you. Is it easier to believe something positive or negative about yourself? Some would say it is easier to be negative. I don't think so. After a class recently that I taught on mental health development someone asked me that question. Why was it easier to believe the negative than the positive?

---

*"Breaking away from some of the
external things that define us won't bring
7 years of bad luck"*

I thought for a moment and told her that I believe that from an early age we are trained in fear from our parents and others in authority over us. Don't run you might slip. Don't do this and don't do that. Obviously some of that was good advice but did you ever hear someone say go ahead and run through the house, you might get faster and win the Olympics one day. Most of what we were taught was a one sided coin. So I believe that our images and thought process is shaped from an early age that seems to be slanted to the negative and not the positive. As we grow up we question whether or nor that is real and look for ways to prove that it is. If we believe that that the world is a cruel place then trust me we will find many examples in our experiences that will what I call anchor that belief in us. Later we will talk about layered belief systems and why they are difficult to change.

There is only one I in Image

I want to talk to you a minute about the ego and how it affects our image of ourselves. In one way the ego can be defined as the part of us that considers ourselves as separate from each other and from our Source, infinite intelligence, or God. Ego also sees our own needs as greater than that of anyone else around us because the focus is on us either in a negative or positive way.

People who are ego driven can have a distorted self image in the positive, the negative or both. I had a lady in one class that if you ask her how she is doing, who she is, how is the weather or anything you will get a litany of her problems, pains, surgeries etc. Her description of herself is one of my pain is greater than your pain so pity me and give me your attention. She constantly interrupts the class coming and going putting on back braces and complaining. This is a sad life.

I took a minute to talk about the ego because it is important to our overall development. It is the I in image. Some believe that the ego must die; I don't believe that but I do believe that there are selfish, self-centered parts of us that have to be sacrificed and denied. I believe the ego must be well formed before it is diminished or lost.

There is only one I in Image; its the ego and you have to decide to make a fundamental decision in life if you want to live a self centered life of living to fulfill your own desires to the detriment of others or to live with a purpose larger than yourself.

You are the keeper of your own image and how you interpret your life's events as well as the direction of your path. The I in image is you; you who must make significant choices in your life that can not be relegated to someone else. You must begin to live an introspective life of self awareness and discovery; a life that embraces change and responsibility. Above all else it must grow into a life of purpose, fulfillment and service.

"Too many rules"

The following is a story told by Ayub Fleming.

I was meeting with someone recently who had a non-profit ministry, was a lawyer in another city but moved and changed careers. She is an attractive and intelligent woman that seemingly could do anything that she wanted to. I was working with her and another family member to help develop their organization when I started noticing that she looked at her future with much trepidation and hopelessness.

The change in her career was leaving a law firm and becoming the one thing that she loved to do and that was to teach. As you know the salary between being a lawyer and teacher is quite substantial. So sticking with her decisions through the financial struggles was not easy much less the criticism from her family.

In talking to her it was difficult to see herself in any other way than someone who was unworthy of a lot of the success that she thought she was able to achieve. Her problems were consuming her; she had little in the way of hope of changing her life, much less that of others.

In meeting with her and talking with her, her pain was marked by physical nervousness, self condemning speech and a focus on how anything of value would get done in her life rather than focusing on the greater questions of what and why. Her ego has isolated her from her Source, her authentic self, and from really feeling loved and appreciated. Her image of herself and the possibilities of the future are distorted.

This lady is a Christian who attends church faithfully and even teaches in bible study and ministers to other *women, but she herself feels broken. While I am not sure of all the drama in her past life that has caused the formation of this negative image and ego driven life, I was sure that who I saw in front of me; a bright intelligent woman was not the image reflected in the challenges of her life.*

After talking to her for sometime we traced some of the issues back to an alcoholic father. Much of her professional career was because someone else challenged and pushed her to become something other than what she felt gave her a since of purpose; being a lawyer was something she never like nor enjoyed. During that conversation when confronted by who she really desired to be, she confessed that she really wanted to teach. The personal expression of teaching is who she really was.

Developing a true picture of you, values, desires and talents as well as the possibilities of the future is critical to building a great life. It is difficult at best to experience real success when you don't think well of yourself or feel good about the possibilities of your life. I think this person is extremely capable and has a bright future. One that I sincerely hope reflects and resonates in the life of many. She has had a profound affect on me.

I have met people with the social skills of a mother badger protecting her young on a hot day in Tucson Arizona with one glass of water left. Their need to always be right and feeling that they are better than anyone else leaves ultimately to loneliness and an empty life.

Our ego before it can be surrendered has to be well defined and developed. So I am not advocating being

Ghandi from the womb. What I am saying is that the path of our lives leads inward and downward and not upward and outward for the things of true meaning and value. Sometimes you have to have something to loose to understand loss. The image that is distorted by ego is the first mirror that needs to be broken.

When we have a reoccurring speech patterns, actions, and projected images we develop habits and lifestyle that many times is self destructive. Let me explain further. Again when we have significant events happen in our life we determine whether this was a good or bad experience for us and we look for the cause of it. Some times we don't accurately evaluate what caused the pain, this is why we can make the same mistakes over and over again because we don't have an accurate correlation between our decisions and experiences.

We can and often do develop thought processes that don't give us the results we want. They manifest in the type of relationships we have, jobs we choose, and also manifest in the words we choose to describe ourselves, others, and the world around us. We develop patterns.

What we really need sometime to put our selves on a healthier path that is more in line with truth of our lives is to interrupt the patterns that produce negative results in our life. Let's examine a few ways to do that.

Change the Experience.

One of the quickest ways to change your long term habits and patterns is to make a stark contrast in what you experience. You have to do quick short irregular things that you don't normally do to break patterns. When you notice that you are one of your routines quickly to something physical that you would not normally do. This will help create a pattern interrupt.

In order to make long term changes you can use the same technique but make planned decisions to add new experiences to your daily routine. This is not just adding a new route to work, but stop along a new route and get coffee at a place you have never been before. Adding new experiences in your life constantly changes the landscape of your beliefs and thoughts because beliefs are formed by significant events. New experiences can challenge or change long held beliefs.

Journaling

Journaling is an incredible way for you to begin to understand the complex thought process that you have about everything in your life and begin to actively shape your life rather than passively live your life.

Writing your thoughts and feelings gives expression to your subconscious in a way that is not possible through conscious thought. If you will begin to journal, write, and plan on a regular basis you will open yourself to a whole new world of understanding how you are making the decisions that you are and experiencing the life you are today.

You will begin to examine how you think and feel and can make shifts in thought that can be very powerful. You also will release a creative side maybe in business or poetry that you may not know existed.

I think of the mind much like a huge filter. Our minds probably filter more information that is deemed useful that it actually stores into long term memory. You can also think of the mind as a huge file cabinet. Storing and categorizing tons of information that form belief systems or associated files. The mind organizes these associations into references so when you meet someone or experience something you have a reference or a pre-determination of what this person, thing, or experience means to you. Sometimes it can be a good determination sometimes prejudice and bigotry based on previous experiences or teachings that go unchallenged.

Journaling allows you a window into those files as well as I believe and opportunity to tap into a more universal consciousness that larger than us as individuals. It's an opportunity to become more self aware and make small corrections in your thought process as well as releasing your creative and giving voice to the previously impossible.

I want to take a moment and talk about 3 mirrors that reflect back images of the past that can be debilitating. These three mirrors reflect in part most of the images we most see in ourselves.

I Am My Things

This mirror that distorts our true image of self is the thought that I am my things. Many images that we get from society at an early age as well as what we are taught is that success and value is measured by what we own. In truth this value has a lot to do by what owns us. A life that strives to own material things as its only gauge of worth is not much of a life at all. Seeking an existence that is valued by money and external things will never be satisfied. Only a life seeking its purpose and intention has a chance of fulfillment. There are too many testimonies of those who have come before us to prove that this is true and that this path no one will escape.

"In Truth value has a lot to do by what owns us"

How many times have we seen athletes and entertainers have some of the finest things money can buy. Cribs (crib is a house for those of you over 50), cars, jewelry, and yes women or men. All of these are accessories that become outward definitions of ones status and worth. To not have them means that you are not a baller (someone who can buy the things in life that they want and spend money on others, this term was first associated with athletes particularly basketball players – again for those of you over 50).

In some socioeconomic stratus this means that you don't get the girl, for some it's the right school, house, Benzo (Mercedes Benz – I won't say it), or the right portfolio. You are not allowed in certain social circles.

This need for outward things to define our image of ourselves as successful has driven many people to lie, cheat and prostitute themselves for that significance and others to financially destroy their lives to maintain an image that is a thinly veiled mirage.

You can not now nor ever create or maintain an image by what you have, you are not your belongings. I like what Suzie Orman has to say about money. One of her Laws of Money if that you are more powerful than your money. Things can be corrupted, corroded, and deteriorate. They don't last and so the drive to accumulate more is only a lustful unfulfilling way to determine your value.

A better determination of success is someone who has a worthy goal for their life and pursues that goal with planning and passion. If they pursue that goal with great focus and effort they will achieve it. If it is a worthy use of your life then you are successful.

I have pursued many things in my life without achieving great monetary reward, but having spent my life in a meaningful way, many times serving others has brought more gratification than the money could have every brought me.

You are not your things.

I am My Past Mistakes

In teaching people about personal development, we have a section in our program that is called "Living the Max Life", that is for mental health. I know we always have that question of does mental health mean that you are a little crazy. No but sometimes you can drive yourself well down that road. We look at mental health the same way we look at physical or financial health. Many times we can be sick but functional. We feel the chronic sickness and weakness of the body and without getting it checked it slowly breaks down.

When I started teaching the program I observed that so many people had such a low opinion and ultimately such a distorted image of themselves that they literally lived up to or down to that image that was created in their mind. I was working with a friend who invited me to speak about homeownership and mentoring programs to a small church in Central Florida. In talking to them and speaking to them about their dreams and goals, we were shocked how broken the women were and that they had very little sense of themselves and what they were capable of.

One of the most powerful indicators of image was that they felt that they were worthy of nothing because of the past mistakes that they have made. The past mistakes had crippled them, has defined them and they could not be accepted because of what they have done. It did not help that there are cultural traditions that they are to be subservient and not see themselves as having the same opportunities as men.

This is a hard subject for me to speak on and remain objective because I believe that women can do anything that men can do; without some physical limitations that are obvious. The men and women from my culture have distinct roles and a great deal of our lives is spent both excusing it and defending it.

Going back to ego, that if you're past is separating you from the forgiveness that you need and the love of God and others than you are alone and crippled. Remember ego separates you from others because it says that you are not connected and that your needs are greater than the needs of others. When you see yourself and begin to believe and act as if you are connected to others but mentally to the things you need then you will see the fruit of those new beliefs manifest in your life.

If you are your past mistakes, then you can not change, because you certainly can not change the past. Consciously we know that we are not our mistakes but inside we feel that way, our beliefs and the references in our lives support the failure that we see in the mirror.

You are not your mistakes, your past nor does any one thing you have done define you. If you have paid for your mistake and learned from the past, learn to forgive yourself and others and move on.

I have made plenty of mistakes and learning to forgive myself and move forward has been a challenge and I have learned tough lessons along the way. Learning to forgive is one of the greatest paths to freedom. Un-forgiveness keeps you bound to that experience, mistake or bad decisions. Practice forgiveness of yourself and others. This does not mean that you act like it never happened and continue in the same behavior or allows other to. It means that you extend grace where none is deserved and you find peace and freedom from these images where none existed.

I am who people say that I am

I am who people say that I am may be the biggest deception of all. When people in authority over us or people that we want affection from criticize us or demean us we begin to embrace that as part of our identity. We embrace the labels of others at times because when you are young people in authority over us provide for us. They provide the essentials things in life to us and defying them brings ridicule and at an extreme harsh punishment.

We often adopt the labels of our friends and people we associate with because we want to belong to the tribe. The old saying going along to get along has hurt all of us to some degree. Our tribal nature of forming groups and sticking together has allowed man to survive in times past but unexamined can slow the development of our own identity or destroy it all together. Recently in a Living the Max Life class one of our senior women after practicing the art of journaling came to the stark realization that she had never known or expressed who she was in over 65 years of life. Her whole identity was wrapped up in living up to or down to the labels placed on her by someone else.

It was sad for all of us to see the light bulb finally come on after all these years and the loss of her youth. She did however find that she had a beautiful talent for writing. At her advanced age she had committed to writing a journal for the first time and allowing her soul to search new vistas and mountains in which to soar.

Even trying to live up to the expectations of others at any young age or trying to be perfect to please someone else can be extremely damaging to the psyche. It is natural to live up to or down to the expectations of others. Learning to live in small tribes means that we have to fit in. However, when the tribe means to diminish you in order for the unit to stay together at some point you must leave the tribe in order to survive, flourish, or become what you were meant to be.

To mature is our natural state. What I mean is that in most circumstances you grow until you outgrow the circumstances and many times the relationships you are in. When you married and one person grows through study and self investment and one does not. Trust me you have serious problems coming in the marriage. It is natural if you continue to grow to become restless and uneasy in your daily life. That restlessness is telling you that something has changed; many times it is a sign that we have out grown our jobs, friends, roles in relationships, and yes even the tribes we belong to. It can be the small voice growing louder and more forceful to us to embrace change and reject the world view thrust upon us.

Ultimately no matter what we see in the mirror we have old tapes assimilated into our unconscious playing over and over again into many experiences and relationships defining us by someone else's words and standards. We project our past experiences both for good and bad into future experiences.

A person who believes they can overcome because of past history of overcoming will believe they can in the future because they have references, so it is for failure as well.

You have to become the voice that speaks into your life internally and defending yourself externally at times. You have to become the prophet in your life that speaks great things into your present and future. If you let someone else label and define you then they are controlling you and in some circumstances living vicariously through you.

You are not the voice of others, you have your own unique voice that needs to be heard and that needs to guide your life. Replace those old tapes with affirmations that you do daily and even stronger incantations that you do as a routine to engage your beliefs and that uses your physiology in a way that creates powerful emotional states. In making changes and reinforcing ones you already have you have to learn how to master the use of your body. One thing women do well is when we want to feel better we change our hair style or color. It adds change that we can identify with when we look in the mirror. Learning to master the use of you physiology can help you master making changes in your life. We will talk more about this later.

I don't allow critics in my life anymore. I do allow people to critique my work as well as find people to be accountable too. You may say well what is the difference? Let me explain. A critic is someone who offers an opinion who is not trying to improve your situation but to manipulate the situation for themselves. Some who offer a critique are doing so to improve you or your circumstances. Their advice is valuable and done in love and not in manipulation. Trust me, the two don't sound the same and they don't feel the same. One is empowering even if the advice is tough to hear, the critic is never empowering.

Examine your life and find out where your image is coming from. Are you allowing the media, others, success, promotions, work, family, or things to define you and determine your worth; if you are; start breaking those mirrors and determine that you are the one who is powerful in determining how you will feel and your ability to influence your life.

Be the voice, don't be the victim.

Image Coaching:

Develop a spirit lead life that has a sense of being connected to Spirit, nature, self and others rather than a life that is disconnected by unworthiness or superiority. Start by doing the work of getting to know yourself as well as who you really believe you are and want to be. Decide not to live an ego lead life and look for opportunities to be connected and not separate. Realize that you are a divine expression of Spirit and you are here for a reason larger than your own ego driven needs.

Learn to forgive. It's a decision first that may have to be reinforced many times by reminding yourself that you have forgiven and to let it go. This may take several times before you can accept it and begin to distance yourself from painful memories and people. Forgive and move on.

Whenever you feel strong emotionally about any-thing begin to ask yourself what you believe about the person or situation that makes you feel this way. Many of our decisions and actions are supporting our emotional states. Learn from them and put more empowering thoughts and actions in place to give you more of the results you want.

Become the voice in your life through daily affirma-tions and incantations.

Don't allow critics in your life. Seek mentors and friends you will critique with honor and love.

Before we move on to the next chapter I want to share with you the story of how a Christmas Wish got started.

Why a Christmas Wish

Hello, my name is Wanda I. Perez and I want to share my experience with you. I was born in Puerto Rico. I have 2 sisters and we were raised by my grandparents on a big farm. I remember my childhood as a happy time. I remember my grandparents raised my two sisters and myself along with 13 other children in a 3-bedroom house. I was the youngest child in the house at the time. I was the baby of the family.

I enjoy my life, we did not have much and we struggled for materials things but we had a great family with good values. At that time we made our own toys, cars and we did play with each other and neighboring kids as well. We were a strong family; at the time we were happy but poor by the standards of many.

I do not remember celebrating Christmas since that tradition was not in Puerto Rico. I do remember celebrating the 3 King's day starting on January 6. In the 3 Kings celebration you took a shoebox and put grass and some water for the Kings and the camels that would come to visit you. My grandmother always told us not to expect anything because the Kings had too many poor kids to go and give gifts too. Sometimes they ran out of gifts, and so they could not get to us that year. I remember year after year I cut my grass, put water and woke up next day to see the shoe box empty. I thought, wow, the camels ate the grass and drank the water on their journey. We lived far and the 3 Kings must have run out of gifts. I never gave up I did continue putting my grass and water underneath the bed. With no success but always with the vision that one-day the 3 Kings will take a short cut and get to my house.

I remember watching the stars and thought about the story that my grandmother always told us that when the 3 stars aligned together the 3 Kings will bring us the gift. I remember that night I looked at the sky and saw the 3 stars aligned, I told my sisters that tonight the 3 Kings will come and bring us the gifts we want, so lets put fresh water and a lot of grass because they are going to be very hungry. Yes they finally came to my home, but the only thing they left me was a candy and underwear. I cried because I could not understand why they took a short cut and they could not bring me the doll I wanted. My grandmother explained that 3 Kings did not have enough and that they must have run out of gifts.

I do remember that same day someone took the time to collect gift and go out to the country and spread them out to the needy, that day a lady handed me a doll and everyone in my house received toys. We were so happy and she said we come representing the 3 Kings. I was so happy that day. In the years to come this same lady came to bring us gifts and give us a wonderful holiday. In Puerto Rico we call them festivals.

I grew up and understood what my real situation in the house was, even we had a big farm we were lacking of money to do other things and Christmas was one of them. I promise myself that when I grew up I was going to do what that lady did, help families who were in need to celebrate their Christmas.

For me Christmas is a time of being with the family and friends and share the laughs of the children opening their presents. I know there are a lot of kids waiting for Santa or 3 Kings to bring them a little bit of joy on Christmas. For one day you could forget your needs, sadness, and stress that are in your life.

For more than 15 years I have been spreading hope out there providing kids with their wish list for Christmas. In 2005, WP Foundation Inc. was born with the mission to "transition lives with love". With the commitment to raise money and collect gift for the kids, to spend time with these kids and families and to let them know that there is hope. I know their circumstances may not change in an instance, but one minute of hope in the life of a child is very important for me, as well as for them. One day I was in the same situation, it was almost 45 years ago when some stranger handed me my first doll and that doll changed my life and gave me a message of hope.

I have partner with the Coalition for the Homeless and it is my 6th year that we adopt families and provide them with their wish list.

I cannot reach out to these families and kids if it wasn't with the support of generous people that have the same heart to help make a difference. I am thankful that I did not stay focused on what I did not have but in what I can give.

WP Foundation Inc. will transition families and kids with love. One day we won't see them anymore, but some of them will continue our legacy the same way someone started with me and they will continue it. This is a personal touch with no ending.

As we grow I know that WP Foundation Inc. will expand our services and address the impediments that keep people from moving forward to creating a life worth living. Now, it starts with touching people and giving them hope in a season that holds so little for so many.

CHAPTER 3

REFLECTIONS

"What we experience on the Outside is a direct Reflection of what we are inside"

unknown

I was looking in a mirror the other day and thought to myself that the mirror must be mistaken. I could see new wrinkles and gray hair that I did not see the other day. Something must be wrong with the mirror; I know that I have not changed so it must be the mirror. I cleaned it but the same image kept showing up. I guess I am getting older.

Reflections are one of the truest sense of how we see ourselves; what is reflected back is factual to what is represented. The part that makes the image distorted is the interpretation of what we see. When we are faced by challenges we see ourselves in the problem. If I have a financial crisis that I am facing I see myself as either capable of fixing it or incapable of changing it. I may see myself as wealthy or having to make some hard decisions to survive. In some cases people make decisions that cause them to loose themselves all together.

In real life the only fun house mirrors that we played in as a kid that made us look fat, skinny, short or tall do exist in our minds. They are the perceptions and filters in which we look at life. When we are determined or have a tendency to see things a certain way no matter what, its like a colored stone that changes the way the whole world looks to us. We have to learn to be more open minded about perceptions and less entrenched in who is right or wrong but leave room for the dialogue to truly understand the position and opinions of others. Sometimes the dialogue is with us. I know; easier said than done.

The interpretation of what we see is a complex matrix of thoughts, feelings, questions, evaluations, and imagination that creates an image that we either live up to or down to. Learning to correctly interpret the images that represent us and others is the first step to wholeness.

Interpretation has a lot to do with someone's world view. Earlier we talked about having predispositions on how things work. When we formulate a paradigm or map of the world we decide how the world works and if it is a creative place of possibilities or a place of impossibilities and just fate. When we stop asking new questions and questioning our own paradigms we fall into a map that may be an old map that no longer exists. The landscape of life changes and we must learn to be flexible in our thinking so we can change with it.

Go back and rethink your position on certain people as well as your view on subjects like money, religion, and politics. Be willing to listen to another point of view and dare I say open your self up to new experiences; as long as it does not violate your moral code or values. The new experiences and your evaluation of them just may enlarge your map to a new and broader world and one that is brighter and less judgmental.

"When we stop asking new questions
and questioning our own paradigms we fall
into a map that may be an old map
that no longer exists"

Confrontation

Have you ever heard people saying that they don't like confrontation? One of the reasons why they don't like confrontation is how they see themselves in it. For some they hate the confrontation because they really see themselves weak and afraid. Loosing the acceptance and perceived respect or love they have taken time to build is not worth the confrontation and possibly loosing that relationship with someone else.

The fact is that our problems and successes create for us opportunities for us to see ourselves in the problem as we are reflected back to us. We can clearly see our reflection in how we respond to circumstances and our speech patterns. When you are afraid of confronting your problem you are afraid of confronting yourself. You perceive that you are powerless to confront and change the problem for your good. Ignoring the problem is ignoring an opportunity for personal growth and development. Thinking that a problem or situation will just go away on its own is naive and sometimes reckless.

Confrontation of self raises the possibility of forced change. If I see myself for what I am now I am responsible for change. Change may bring tough choices to go against entrenched and strongly held beliefs and relationships. Remember many times our paradigm has been, it's easier to go along to get along. Continual questioning and confrontation of self is the path to continued growth.

I asked someone once why they did not confront the problem they were facing. I won't go into details but this was a serous problem that meant they were facing jail time. The answer the person gave me was astounding. They said that they thought if they ignored it, it would go away. Well you may say that this is ridiculous and you would be right; it is. Don't we do that everyday when choosing to hide in our mess rather than confronting it? We wait until the small scratch perceived as a wound gets infected and we are faced with cutting our leg off to even think about change.

The reason that the person did not want to confront their problem is that they did not think nor feel that they could have an influence over it. If they hid long enough maybe the coast would be clear and they could come out again from hiding. The person is strong in many areas of their life but weak where they have evaluated from experience that they have little or no influence to change their circumstances. This person is one of the brightest and most talented people that I know. Tragically they are a classic example of a compromised life, failure, misery, and hopelessness.

Confrontation is a part of life. When we create we confront obstacles that cause us to think, adapt and overcome. We also confront problems that challenge us to think at a higher level that caused the problem. When we shy away from confrontation we are saying that we can't and so we don't.

In your experiences as you get older each one gives you an opportunity both good and bad to interpret the reflection of yourself when you face it and accept responsibility for changing the circumstance. The same is true in empowering situations. If you have worked hard and accept the rewards that come along with success then the reflection that you and others see is someone successful, strong, and resilient and a person who has learned to trust them and overcome obstacles.

Accepting Responsibility

The main word here is responsibility. That word means that you have the ability and to what measure you can respond to something. This is partially based on self image. Accepting responsibility has to be done first to the degree that it is your responsibility to respond to something. This means that we all know that we can not always control what happens to us but we all can accept responsibility for our response to our experiences both good and bad. Many of our problems have come to us by others who have not fully or even partially accepted responsibility.

It also means with something has gone right or wrong that we make an honest assessment to our role. If it is wrong then we own up to it and take the appropriate action to correct it and learn from it so it does not happen again.

Let's talk a minute about and talk about *locus of control.* This is psyche term that basically means how you interpret your role and responsibility to the things that affect your life.

It's my fault

It's never a healthy position to take that no matter what it's your **entire** fault. There is a natural disposition for some that says it's my entire fault if it's wrong. This person believes that the world revolves around them. It may not seem so because it is acted out in the negative but this person is self absorbed and self centered. This person also sees things in absolutes and has very little room for the opinion of others. The typical question that they ask internally is what's wrong with me?

In most circumstances in our life as adults there is almost always some responsibility on our part. Many times we accept too much responsibility and apply no responsibility to others. This can lead to us to be neurotic. In healthy relationships or circumstances each person must become responsible for their share of the mistake in order for the relationship to move forward and trust remain in tact.

Great teams have individual players that accept responsibility for their role both for their own success and for that of the team.

It's your fault

This is the type of person who never sees anything as their fault. They don't allow for any type of true analysis, they don't have to; it's not their fault. How many times in your life have you seen someone no matter what just accept no responsibility for their condition? In this position it is nearly impossible to change.

The person that I mentioned earlier that thought their problem would go away if they ignored it has this same locus of control. This person never accepts responsibility for the condition of their life.

The problem is that this person does not correctly associate their decisions that they make and the ones they avoid are the cause of the condition of their life. They think that other people are treating them unfair and that life is unfair to them. They don't associate decisions and hard work with success. They look for the breaks and handouts in life to get what they want.

As Dr. Phil says, "you can not change what you won't acknowledge". I could not agree more.

It was written; its God's will

This person accepts no responsibilities for their actions and ignores key elements of God's word when it suits them. Clearly God specifies his moral will clearly in His word, His specific will as to choices that we are to make is not always so clear. There is never a place for our outlook to suggest that everything that happens has no bearing on the decisions we make daily. Destiny is the study of cause and affect, reaping and sowing; wishing our responsibility away does not absolve us of making choices.

This position sees as mere by standers in our life and something even less than victims. If everything is written and we have no influence than we have NO choice. If this is your religious belief than you should never be happy or unhappy because you have completely surrendered your life to this belief.

The healthiest way to look at situations is to assess your responsibility of yourself and others and respond to that situation based on your ability. If you need help to correct or find a solution to the situation, get help. It's always unhealthy and detrimental to your life to be completely invested in the outlook of any one way. Many times it's a combination of two or three points of view.

God does have a will for us. I believe it is His moral will that is the clearest. I think there is a real concept of serendipity or synchronicity but I feel these occurrences are rare and it's the decisions we make and what we believe that affects our lives the most.

Image Coaching:

Accept confrontation as a part of life. Confrontation is powerful and must be a part of your success paradigm. Confrontation does not mean you have to be angry or belligerent but it means that you face the issue and develop strategies to overcome. In some relationships it means that you don't allow others to manipulate and define you and you put things in proper perspective.

Accept a healthier outlook on life that places roles and responsibilities where they truly should be placed. Don't take the blame for something that you did not do. Being noble does not always mean falling on the sword. Holding others and yourself accountable is a healthy position to take.

Accept the fact that your decisions and beliefs affect your life more than anything else. Seek God's will but understand it is His moral will that is best defined. Pray, meditate, but then act. Faith without works is dead.

CHAPTER 4

THE MATRIX OF SELF IMAGE

"The quality of an individual is reflected in the standards they set for themselves"
                    Ray Kroc (1902 - 1984)

The Self Image Matrix is a term that we use in the Living the Max Life program to understand how we mentally develop an image of ourselves. How do we form patterns of thought into belief systems that ultimately developed a self concept, esteem, and image of ourselves and the world around us?

Self-Image Matrix

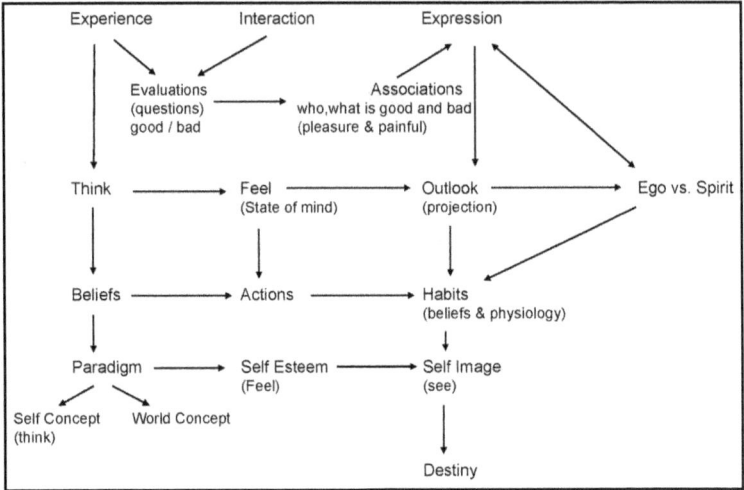

Experience

The experiences in our lives are the first step in how our self image is shaped. Our self image influences the decisions we make and ultimately does have some affect on our path that we choose and our destiny. The things that happen to us throughout our lives and how we interpret them have a profound effect on the direction of our lives and what we achieve or don't achieve. My early experiences shaped how I thought and felt about myself and later crystallized into an image that was impossible to get beyond until it was exposed.

My image of myself was at times one of a victim. I remember so many beatings almost daily that I saw myself largely a victim of circumstances that I could not control. I learned to push in the pain until many times I exploded with anger. The continued beatings, mistreatment and my upbringing as a child also caused me to live most of my life in fear.

My image was also that of a boy since I was repeatedly called that. It is not that I considered myself male but I took on those traits as a woman because it was a form a rebellion. If you are going call me a boy then I am going to act like one. I can't tell you how many fences I climbed and things that I did with my boy cousins and my sisters. I was the mischievous one that was always getting injured from doing things that I was not supposed to do. I saw myself as strong and forceful but also weak and victimized.

Experiences from birth begin to shape what we think, how we feel and ultimately how we view ourselves, others, and the world. I believe from conception a child can know intuitively whether or not it is loved or rejected. This is reinforced depending on how the child is reared, whether it is held, breast fed, or left alone and ignored. We are not arguing about the merits of breast feeding but the larger discussion of connection and intimacy. The physical bond with a child from minutes after the birth to the first hug of graduation even into college can shape the rest of a child's life.

I remember my child hood was a happy one when I was with my grandfather but after eight years old when I was introduced to my birth father that was to change. My first experience was me and my sisters being taken on a vacation. We were not told where we were going or for what reason. I remember walking out of the gate in New York and my grandmother introducing me to this woman and saying this is your mother. I remember saying to her this is not my mother and with that, this women that I did not even know slapped me. I did not know what to think at that moment but I knew I was in trouble. How could my grandmother and father who raised, loved, and protected me expect me to understand the complicated issues of adults?

As we were introduced to my father a new life began to emerge but it was not real to me. The only parents that I had known now were leaving me. After a few days my grandmother was taken back to the airport I fully expected to leave with her. She told me that I could not go and that I had to stay. As I held on tight to her leg, I was pried off and this time beaten in the terminal. The only mother that I had known and the farmhouse that had been my home was gone. The next ten years of my life would be marked by abuse and molestation.

When something happens to us that is traumatic it creates a sensation of either pain or pleasure; pain in the sense that we want to avoid it and pleasure in the sense that we want to repeat it or have it happen again. We also ask questions in the process of evaluating it to find out why it occurred. It's very easy in these moments to misdiagnose the problem. Some can internalize the beatings and say that I deserved it, it must be my fault. Others can drift into developing other personalities to deal with the circumstances.

It was not long before the beatings began by my father. It seemed right from the beginning I was the target and not my sister. I kept wondering why me? Why did this new man in my life; that I now know as my real father who had abandoned us when we were young hated me?

My mom at times tried to help me with the beatings by putting extra clothes on me before my father would arrive at home for the frequent beatings when he had been drinking. My mother and I were the only two persons in the house who were beaten. I came to resent my sisters and my mother for not protecting me and more for them watching the abuse my mother took and yet they said nothing. Maybe I was not worth protecting. Maybe I was a boy and needed to be strong like one. These were the questions that I answered that created a paradigm for my life and influenced my actions for more than 40 years.

Your mind records the event but begins to ask the question at that moment, what caused it so I can avoid it or recreate it. This process of deciding what things mean is called an evaluation. I can talk in these terms today but how does a child understand why they are being abused? To make it stop the child will both try everything to be free from the abuse or accept it and bond with their captor. No matter the decisions to cope the ramifications will be felt over a life time as many of the scars are emotional, mental, and not just physical.

Sometimes the question of avoiding pain can cause us to exhibit behaviors that are not in our best interest though it's a coping mechanism; some have great long term consequences. Many times I did not properly evaluate why my grandmother and later my real mother left me, why was I being beaten. I struggled with issues of whether or not they loved me and what love meant.

I know I was a precocious little kid who was always getting in trouble but I did not deserve this. I was always playing with the boys, jumping fences, always hiding my injuries so I would not get spanked. I never knew what my father's background was or why he did the things that he did. Why did he hate me? I could not ask the one person who could answer the question so I had to make my own assumptions.

We begin to associate people and things as being the cause of what is good or bad for us even at a very young age. Sometimes we learn that destructive behavior can get us the attention we want, so we do it because the attention that we want fulfills a deeper need of acceptance or significance. Our need for security, love, affection, etc., must be met. As a child you don't understand things like locus of control or character flaws you just know something bad is happening to you and you are powerless to stop it.

Experiences throughout our lives can either support or contradict our current belief systems as what are called references or anchors. They can add to our belief systems if we have no reference or prior experience. The way we evaluate our experiences can also cause mixed emotions about them. Experiences can cause us to feel both pain and pleasure are called mixed nuero-associations meaning they have two different meanings and produce opposite or mixed feelings at the same time. The family members who were there to protect you don't; you are molested but you can't tell anyone and in the end many times we were called liars or it must have been our fault. The mixed feelings came because this was my father, my sisters and mother. This was now the only family I knew. If they would not love me then who would? I have to survive and find a way to love and be loved by them; by someone.

The experiences that I had at an early age did shape my life and what I started to associate many people with pain. The association most often felt with pain was my relationships with men. As I grew older I had many experiences that anchored my beliefs and dysfunctional relationships and I began to have experiences in my life that challenged my thoughts and beliefs. This is why we are not our past and we have a great opportunity to change our present and future reality. It is because our experiences and the way we evaluate them can change and so can our lives.

You may ask how can I go back and redefine my experiences. First we have to put the blame where it counts. As a child you are not to blame for they abuse you suffered at the hands of adults. Second you can have it fixed in your mind that the past is not the only determination of the future and that whatever has happened to you it does not have to control your ability to grow and create the life that you want to live.

Ask yourself what I had to believe about the circumstance in which I found myself to develop the belief system that I have today. What can I believe about the circumstance that can create a more powerful future for me today? Can I use my experience not to disqualify me but can it qualify me to be a help to others going through the same thing?

You can go back and try to figure out why and though you can't justify what was done you may find reasons that allow you to forgive and or say that it was not my fault that it happened this way. I am not my past so though this happened to me, I don't have to take the blame. I can accept the past learn from it, grow past it and move on. I am not my past and it does not define me. I also suggest that you consider getting professional help if you have suffered significant trauma in your life and need help. It's difficult to process these events in your life and find freedom but you deserve to be free and live a fulfilled life. I hope that my story if not giving you the answers will inspire to seek help and get it.

Interaction / Dialogue

I believe it is true that our experiences can change our thoughts and our beliefs; but we don't have these experiences in a vacuum. As we continue on the image matrix I wanted to share the second concept with you; a concept that I believe that everyone shares in their experience.

The next thing that I believe is common to all people is dialogue, interaction, or communication with people, and our environment. When I talk about dialogue to simplify the meaning I just mean our communication with someone or something. It's what we give and take away from the experience.

Our experiences change us because we come in contact with something and take away something from that interaction. It can reinforce or challenge our beliefs. It's like making new friends who open your mind to new possibilities because of the communication and change in experiences from what you are used to. In the dialogue we learn from each other and our environment but there is an exchange on many levels. What we learn can be both good and bad, sometimes we are affirmed in the conversation and sometimes we are not.

In my interaction with my family at a young age my father taught me that is was never safe around men and that he did not value me for who I was. My mother taught me that you had to protect yourself sometimes at great expense. I had male relatives who tried to have sex with me as a child and at a young age I was molested. There were many experiences that anchored my beliefs about protecting me from men. I see one particular uncle sometimes in other men as they approach me in a certain way; it triggers fear, anger and resentment in me. Also my parents sent me with this uncle on several occasions and allowed me to be alone with him. They violated my trust and did not protect me. My primary question in my life was how I protect myself from men.

The dialogue or experience with these men taught me a lot about men as I projected my past pain and insecurities on my future relationships.

In the dialogue we can learn that we are being listened too and that it's a safe place to communicate and be ourselves. If we are communicated with in this fashion then we see ourselves and our opinion as valuable. If we are not heard, valued for our opinion or pushed aside in roles that make us seem invisible then we learn that we are not valued. Our struggle to be heard can cause to make decisions and act out in ways that are contrary to whom we are and what we value; but at least someone is paying attention.

It's hard to change some childhood experiences and make them positive. If our interaction with others and life is harsh then we can learn that we are of no value and that the world is not a safe place to express yourself. This lack of or negative self concept, esteem and ultimately image can be devastating to the growth and expression of the individual.

The opposite is true as well. Some parents want to love so much that they relinquish the role of parenting to one of a friend; where over indulgence and protecting their children from all harm and from making decisions that are natural to growing up and essential to becoming an adult can be just as harmful. Many psychologists would say to the parent who treats their children like this are not loving them at all but feeding into their own unmet needs to be accepted and loved by their children.

Interaction can be experienced not only in conversation but our interaction with others can be that of great support, love, nurturing, but it can also be of abuse both physically and emotionally. One if supported can lift us to great heights because we believe in ourselves and have a positive self image. The other can cause self loathing behavior that creates an invisible ceiling for ourselves of what is possible. When taken to extremes destructive behaviors can result and range from compulsive disorders to drug use to illegal activities like prostitution. It could be argued that a marriage without love for the sake of provision with little voice and expression is a legal and accepted form of prostitution.

I know that sounds harsh but so many women marry with little identity and completely disappear in the marriage by assuming roles with little expression of their own voice. When you speak out of a role or responsibility and from the opinion that you have assumed of others and not your own, than you are not speaking for yourself, but someone else. Your voice is not being heard in that conversation. The premise is that you have nothing to add of value. Roles we were told when we were young of being a nurturer and provider are honorable and the greatest gift women have to offer other than procreation; but so many of us die in sorry for so much of our lives and gifts go unexpressed.

Our interaction with others teaches us many lessons in life especially early. As we grow older much like experience our interaction can strengthen our belief systems, add to them, or cause mixed emotions about our beliefs. We can control and limit our interaction with negative people and circumstances. We can decide who and what we want to influence our lives. If we choose empowering interactions with mentors, family, and friends we can have different experiences that can support and promote a better life. We can love our families but it is our responsibility to choose our peers. Your peers are the people in your life that you choose to interact with as they help shape your feelings (esteem) and your paradigm. Your peers have a great deal of influence in your life, choose them wisely. This is why we should be so concerned over the type of peers our children choose as they will have as much if not more influence over them than you will. The choice at some point is ours to make.

I think we can also decide to fill our lives also with interactions of a more spiritual nature through prayer and meditation. This can also be done by making time to slow down and go into deep thought and connect with yourself and God in the quiet. I have a friend who recounts some of his deepest experiences in life were at times when he was alone and quiet. Probably the only times that rival that for him was times spent in Sedona and the Grand Canyon. For myself, my most sacred times always take me back to the mountains.

Expression

The topic of expression is a deep one for me and hard for me to communicate. It is one that I have struggled with the most being both misunderstood and many times rejected. I still struggle with that because English is not my natural language so when my interaction with others depends on communicating with words they don't come out they way I want them to sometimes.

Expressing ourselves, our gifts, talents, skills, and our own unique voice in this world is critical not only to our development but is necessary to fulfill your intended purpose. There is an old saying that one of the greatest tragedy is to die with your music still inside.

As I have grown older (and better looking) it is not until recent that I really had a clue what I was capable of and how unique my voice is in the conversation. Many times through anger I yelled so loud that I could not even hear what I was saying. I have learned to be more empowered by expressing my opinion and living my expression through my vocation, family, and my community work. I still have work to due as I catch myself being triggered by old memories into behaving in a way gets me seen but not heard.

Self expression is purposely entering the conversation of your life. It is the exposure of what is inside you. Our self expression at a young age is affected by what we were taught. Our parents, teachers, and others could have taught us to speak up and give our opinion or to remain silent because we were just children. The expression that I was taught of as a child was very narrow. Young children especially women were not supposed to play like the boys, do this or that. As a young child I saw that I as my sisters was being prepared for our excepted roles as women which came down to being wives and little more than sexual objects for men.

This is not to bash men; we need good men and good relationships with them in our lives. The question is do we know what we want, what we are willing to prepare ourselves for, demand, and be patient and wait for? How often do we jump on the first man that shows us some attention and we dumb ourselves down in order to not make them feel less comfortable or for us to be more desirable to them. Somewhere in the process we slowly and sometimes completely loose ourselves.

Self expression is also identifying yourself by your own definitions and not allowing others to define you or your purpose in this life. Let's talk about that for a minute. We have roles to play and accepted labels that describe what we do. The problem is when others label us they can define and control us. When you don't say who you are and what you are capable of then you are not in the conversation of your own life.

Your life is on auto pilot just accepting and performing in the minstrel show as someone else has defined it. Be the voice in your own life. Educate your self and plan your life to include things that define who you are and want to become.

Expression is releasing your potential and purpose into the world. Something unique was deposited into us all by Spirit with the intention of having that special something released and to be heard in the conversation of life. There are many ways to express you. It may be through poetry, raising your children and sharing your life story with them. It could be running for political office or as a police officer expressing your talents in protecting your community. Whatever the conversation you may enter, your voice must be heard and added to the consciousness of life.

I had a friend who knew a great artist; she painted in oil paint and other mediums. He supported her art including sending her to art school and becoming a certified art instructor under a very famous artist. She had very low esteem and it showed in her painting. If she was in a good mood her paintings were light and vibrant. If she was in a bad or depressed state her paintings were dark and dreary though she almost always painted the same types of subjects.

She had been abused in her marriage until she left her husband and got a divorce. She had also lost her father at a young age and was passed around in the family living with several relatives. She was molested for years not by a male in the family but her aunt.

She was a custodian for years and he assisted her in getting another job in the printing business and trying to get her to put some of her artwork in print. Eventually her negative experiences of her past formed a negative thought process that continued to follow her until she gave up and gave into the limiting beliefs that she had. She returned to what she always described herself to be and that was a cleaning lady. The saddest thing is that neither she nor the world will ever know what beautiful paintings lay inside of her.

I truly believe that when we don't live up to our own potential to express ourselves, talents, and unique gifts that the world is diminished by the lack of music, art, poetry, speeches, inspiration, and love.

Thought

It was once said that the problem with men (people) is that they don't think they conform. This comment was made by Earl Nightingale who was a great motivator. Well I think that statement is very true. The process of thinking is a complicated process of accessing existing data, searching for new data, asking questions, reasoning, and making assumptions about things until we form an opinion.

Our opinion is supported by enough references for what we believe to become fact or our perception of the truth. Our reality is based on our perception of what is true. What may be true to you may not be to someone else. If you don't believe this put a democrat and republican together and maybe throw in a libertarian and bring up almost any subject and watch the sparks fly.

Our experiences begin to form a thought process. Our thought process is how we process and assign meaning to the information from our experiences. Is what we experienced something we heard, saw, felt, or experienced physically? Did it cause us pleasure or pain?

Has someone described you in a certain way that is consistent to what you believe or inconsistent? Our thoughts are how we process events in our life and how we evaluate what they mean to us. It's the process of forming opinions on one hand and using those opinions or perceptions to make decisions.

Our thoughts are also influenced by the process of asking questions and what conclusions we come up with. Questions are powerful because they are part of the reasoning process that seeks to understand. If we don't ask the right questions to the right people then we have to make an assumption(s).

Assumptions usually draw wrong conclusions because they are not based on fact. Even in memory your brain fills in the gaps to tell a complete story. When you generally remember back to child hood you access random bits of information to recall something that happened. When you start to create an image of the event sometimes your mind fills in the gap by creating part of the story. It can seem very real.

Some of the things you remember may not have happened the way you remember them. You can ask other people what they recall from a certain event and their story may not match. At times when witnesses to crimes have been asked what happened the evidence of the investigation does not match the eye witness account. Several people watching the same event can recall completely different things though there may be some or many similarities.

So if you holding onto a self image that could be in part based on something that did not happen or assumptions you had to make then one of the things in your life that affects you the most could be wrong or at least not supported by the facts. When someone calls you stupid, you may accept that over time because you may have enough references to question how smart you really are. If you accepting that has no factual basis you could have achieved much more in your life by challenging the label someone placed on you by seeking out experiences to challenge the notion that you are stupid.

In my example I had to ask myself why my father hated me so much. I was the only one that he would beat no matter what. Sometimes I wondered not just why but why did he seek me out. I was even beaten for things that others did but I was the whipping post. I remember trying to hide myself by switching positions in the dark with my sister to see if he would pick her. I just wanted one night of sleep without the fear of being beaten or actually going through it; somehow he always knew where I was and in his anger my mother and I alone suffered his wrath.

I also had to ask myself how to survive the beatings since my mother never intervened but only defended my father even when he beat her. I remember being able to put my mind somewhere else even as my body suffered such hatred and indignity. As I grew older I was able to stand there and physically take the beatings without any sign of showing pain. This made him even more furious but it became my survival mechanism. Later as I grew up I remember being confronted by men even in offices where I worked with my husband; approached me for sex I would freeze, terrified to protect myself.

I still ask to this day why; with my father having past away and my mother providing no answers I only have assumptions to make and the aftermath of him to clean up the fragments left in my life by his influence. I can only assume why he hated me but I have no answers. The problem is since my father passed away the one person who could answer that question is gone.

The process of assuming is when you can't or don't ask the right questions to the right people about the right things and get the right answers. You mind requires and answer so we assume by picking a logical answer to the question. Sometimes our assumptions help us through the situation and sometimes they create thought processes that can injure us until they are challenged and new more empowering questions can be asked and answered.

Since my father had passed away there was no one to ask. I have decided though to challenge the notion that I was masculine, stupid, and just a whipping post. By not allowing me to be labeled and challenging that labels that were applied and seeking out experiences of love and acceptance so much of my thought process and therefore my life has changed.

Being told something by our parents or someone in authority over us or someone we love can have great influence in our thought process. The way we think and our conclusions can be distorted if our evaluation of our experiences and what is and is not fact is distorted.

Men and women are thinking beings who can also feel. Sometimes what we think and feel can be at conflict. Many times we have to honor the way we feel and express them but we have to be able to ask ourselves is the way I feel true. This process of expressing feelings, asking questions, gathering facts is called reasoning, and it is a powerful tool of shaping the way you think. This is why if you can change they way you think by changing the process as well as the conclusions. You can change the direction of your life.

How can we change the way we think? One of the ways we can is to change our thoughts about of own self image. We can do that by basing it on the outcomes we want in the future rather than our perceived results in the past. You can re-focus your life from what you have experienced in the past to the outcomes you want in the future. Life then is about what you are and what you have decided to become. If you can do this, then you can begin to take more control of your own life. When I was young, I only thought about surviving but gave little thought to which I was becoming or what I wanted to become.

We all have circumstances that we can not control but we can control what we think about them as well as how we will respond to them. I have met many people who have overcome great adversity and have come through it because they determined that they were not going to be broken by them. They would survive for a greater purpose and would overcome to share their experiences and themselves with the world.

Feeling / Emotional State

Many times I am criticized because I speak my mind and for those close to me there is no doubt to the way I feel. I think that is a criticism of a lot of women though I have met many better than me at pretending.

Emotional state is one of those concepts that are an extension of our feelings. When you have powerful feelings like anger or even passion you can a state or lingering affect from the feelings that can alter your decisions and maybe even simple things like perception. Think back to a time when you were really pissed, I mean what they call .38 hot. (For you young folks .38 hot means you are hot like a pistol) Remember that during this time you may have been angry and depressed or resentful, you may have even said and done things that you would not normally do. I can't tell you how many times that has been true for me and learning how to master or create emotional states has allowed me many times to respond to situations clearly and responsibly.

Our emotional state is based on how we feel. Our feelings create powerful states that can affect our decisions. They can move us from the rational mind that thinks to the irrational mind that just reacts. Emotional states are the X factor. Most know that they can make decisions when they are calm and thinking about a situation one way but will make a totally different decision if they are angry or sad. We know this but we don't take much time to change or influence our emotional state or at least look at what state we are in when we make decisions.

Learning to master your emotional state is one of the missing links in living an empowered life. It has been proven that emotional knowledge (quotient) and control can be more important than just looking at intelligence alone. EQ most often is more important than IQ.

Feelings are also intuitive. Many times we can feel when something is wrong. There is no rational explanation that something is off or about to happen but we just feel it. We need to honor our feelings and express them. Journaling is one of the best ways to express your feelings and begin to rationalize them and try to understand why you are feeling a certain way. If you have a strong sense of something sometimes its best to stop and be quiet or for some; pray for an answer.

Why are feelings important?

Feelings shape our lives because we project our feelings onto things that we have evaluated as good or bad. Lets talk about that a minute. When you have gone through the evaluating what something means when you have a significant event in your life; you begin to associate that event or thing with a certain feeling. This is due in part to what it represents to you. When something is represented to you in a certain way and you have anchored that belief about that through experience or knowledge you belief it and associate a feeling with it.

Trust by the time you go through a few puppy loves when you are young and a few frogs when you are older you have well defined belief and feeling when you think about men. Much the same as they say about us; can't live with them can't live without them.

Feelings shape our decisions along with our rational thought process; the way we think and feel sometimes can be at odds. Intense enough feelings about something can override your intellect and cause you to make decisions you would not normally do. There are hundreds of love songs that people can identify with that tell this tale of the feelings of love over ruling our mind that says be cautious something is not right.

So what is state and why is it important? Emotional state goes beyond just a feeling. Emotional state is when 3 things that you do naturally combine to create a state of mind that do affect not only your mood but your decisions.

Well you may ask is what we believe so cut and dry. I would say most of the time no. Belief systems are layered because we have many experiences that sometimes are in conflict in their meaning to us but it's the emotional state and not rational thought many times that is the deciding factor on how we are going to decide, act, or believe.

Emotional State

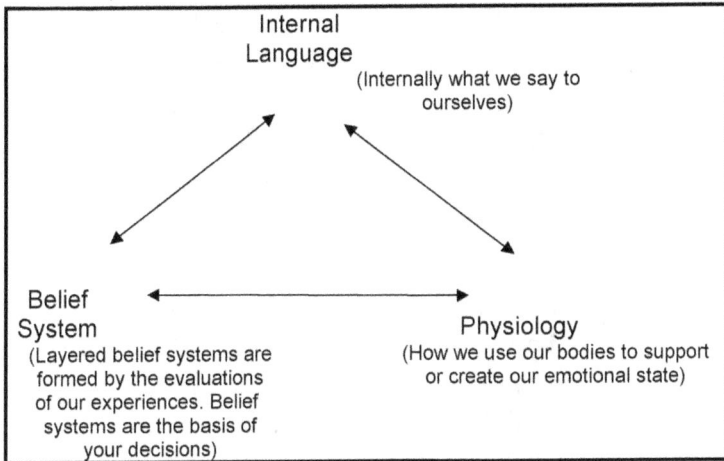

Internal
Language
(Internally what we say to
ourselves)

Belief
System
(Layered belief systems are
formed by the evaluations
of our experiences. Belief
systems are the basis of
your decisions)

Physiology
(How we use our bodies to support
or create our emotional state)

Emotional states are important because when people consider changes that they want to make people think in terms of them wanting to feel different and in most cases to change a behavior. Emotional states do accomplish both of those things.

Emotional States have three factors; belief systems, physiology, and our internal language. Our belief systems are our experiences that have been evaluated and stored in our subconscious mind. Belief systems are layered because we have so many significant experiences that shape what we think and how we feel. Sometimes we have differing beliefs that are accessed in decision making largely depending on how we feel, our values, and the information we may have at hand; however the stronger the emotional state the fewer factors that are considered in making decisions.

For instance faced with the same facts you make one decision when you are in love and a completely different decision when you are angry. In your normal rational state you may evaluate something that you want to buy and walk away because that dress or shoes are not in the budget. If you are angry especially at your significant other you may not only buy one pair but three just too really get them back. Funny how that does work the way we think it will in the moment.

A belief system is much like a drawer within a large file cabinet. The subconscious mind that stores information in the brain is the file cabinet. How you access information and how you decide to use it is largely based on your emotional state. There are also other factors such as filters, meta-programs or dispositions but in the moment it is largely due to your emotional state. Beliefs and emotional states are actively changing all the time. Beliefs due to experiences and emotions due to what we say to ourselves and how we use our physiology.

The basic thing that I want you to get is that you have a set of beliefs that are formed from knowledge and events and anchored by other experiences and events and in your mind proven to be true. These beliefs are associated with feelings and can help create emotional states that affect decisions.

Our physiology is our physical body including our nervous system. Our body and mind is connected in a powerful way through our nervous system. Emotional states are created. That's right created. In order for someone to be happy they have to believe something about the experience or condition. Second they have to do something with their body to support that feeling or they will have a mixed nuero-association. Third they have to create or reinforced that feeling by what they say to themselves and how they evaluate the circumstance they are in or where they perceive that they will be.

Let's slow down for a minute. Think about this. Women who believe that they are sexy and feels that way does not leave it a random thought process. Sexy people express that in how they use their bodies and how they project that with clothes, shoes, make up that creates an image. The opposite is true is someone believes that are ugly. They spend less time on their dress, hair, nails, etc. They way they walk and carry themselves do not project sexiness or confidence either.

If I feel excited about something but use my body in a way that supports depressed feelings then I am having mixed feelings about something. For example if you try to stay unhappy but move your body in a way that you do when you are happy you will not be able to stay sad. The emotional state of sadness will not be able to last if I do the things with my body that I would normally do when I feel good. The opposite is true as well.

Our internal language is what we say to ourselves and how we say it. Our internal language can be affirming or disaffirming and destructive. If you hear depressing news but your reaction is to stand up tall, breathe deeply, and tell yourself something positive about the news then it will be difficult if not impossible to get depressed about it.

Professional athletes after making a bad play either get back in the game or sulk and almost hide hoping they won't be called upon. Dr. Lohrer wrote a book called *Toughness Training for Life* which studies top athletes and what separates them from average athletes when physical stature does not seem to separate them.

He found out that between plays the best athletes would talk to themselves getting them back in the mind set to perform at their peak while other athletes let the pressure get to them. He also noted how they did something between plays like a physical move that got them ready to play again. Top athletes engage their physiology and internal language to excel. You can as well in the game of life.

The more you can combine your internal language, beliefs, and physiology into a strong tool to work for you rather than against you, the more you will be in control in making better decisions and experiencing a more powerful life.

Outlook

In general we all have an outlook on life. I have to admit at times I have been a bit of a pessimist. My confidence in myself was one thing but I always kept finding a way to believe in other people until I continually got disappointed. Some times I ignored warning signs and other times I projected my pain and pessimism into my relationships and circumstances.

Our outlook is our thought process projected into circumstances in faith or fear. Our experiences tell us that certain people, places, and things have a meaning attached either good or bad. In general your experiences then either reinforce or challenge that belief.

How we project our thought process unto circumstances, people, places and things is made up of filters, our disposition, how we frame things and what is called meta-programs. Meta-programs are much like paradigm but more based on the way the brain is actively programmed. These are complex ways that our brain sees and reacts to things. The way we filter information is by deciding what is important to us at the moment. Our filters sometimes keep us from using information that is important to making decisions. We have to pay attention to they way that we and others filter information.

Have you ever had a meeting and someone walk out and want to talk about the meeting? The more they talk the more you wonder what meeting they were in. They can get the simplest facts so mixed up or even worse see what happened through their own agenda that they seemingly missed what happened.

Framing is how we create pictures our boundaries in interpreting what something means. There is an old story about a man who looked out the window and saw this man screaming for help when he saw him he was running but did not seem to be chased by anything. He went back and sat down and again heard the screams. He went back to the window and looked and saw the man running the other direction. Again he saw nothing that would cause this person action so he sat back down. A minute later he heard nothing and being curios of what happened to the wild man he went back to the window and moved closer for a better view and saw the man being eaten by a lion. His limited view only saw a person screaming, since he relied on what he saw which made no sense to him he paid no attention. If he had gotten to a point of a wider view he would have seen the cause of the problem. Sometimes we need to reframe the issues of our lives to understand them.

Our outlook is how we project our beliefs into our circumstances. Understanding how we filter and frame things and our natural reaction to things is essential to adjusting our outlook or at least questioning the way we see things to make sure we get the best vantage possible.

Belief Systems / Paradigm

Continuing to follow the image matrix we have talked about experiences forming the basis our image we hold of our self and the world around us today. Information can also construct image if there is no opposing information available; this becomes your limited experience.

We earlier spoke about interaction and entering into dialogue where we change what we touch and are changed by what touches us; either for good or bad. Then we went on to discuss personal expression which I think could be a whole book by itself. Personal expression breeds confidence and the lack of personal expression breeds self contempt. A person with no voice has no voice in which to be heard. A person who is mute may hear the language but even if he could speak could not speak the language without training. He has never learned to speak with his own voice.

We then talked about the experiences we have; we evaluate by assigning meaning and value to them. Some that bring us pleasure makes us want to understand what caused it and to have it repeated. We begin to associate certain people and things as either good or bad. Sometimes our associations are completely wrong and irrational.

We talked about feelings and what role they play in developing and emotional state and how it affects making decisions. Finally we talked about our outlook on life or how we project our thoughts and feelings into our lives as well as future events.

At the point of projection our belief systems are what are called paradigms or mental models of how the world works. Some are crystallized or what some call concretized meaning they are set like concrete. We would say "written in stone". When they get to this point it takes great events called paradigm shifts to change our minds.

Many of us become inflexible and set in our ways. It is not that we can not change our paradigms but it takes a significant challenge to our beliefs to change them. I am sure you have talked to many people where you know you are wasting your time. You know that soon they are going to hit that brick wall that will change the way they look at things if not they are in for having a flat face. Here are some things that I want you to know about belief systems.

Our belief systems are:

Belief systems are based on experiences and how we evaluated their meaning to us.

Belief systems are fluid because we can have many beliefs sometimes conflicting because our experiences can be interpreted in different ways. Our emotional state(s) accesses our beliefs and influence our decisions.

Belief systems are layered much like a large file cabinet that can contain experiences that support or contradict your thought process. Sometimes both at the same time.

Beliefs are resident memories and not activated outside of external stimulus. Therefore you are not your beliefs, because the definitions of the experiences can be changed along with new associations, affirmations, and incantations that can change your thinking and decisions.

When someone becomes convinced of how his life with turn out or convinced of how the world works then the belief system has crystallized into a mental map. This person will follow that map because to them it is truth. Many times emotional states may not even affect their decisions. They will follow a path disregarding the stop and warning signs not to proceed. Paradigms are very difficult to change and usually are only revealed when there is a crisis.

In order to grow we must seek knowledge with the thought that we don't know everything and that seeking out new knowledge and experiences will continue to change us, our paradigms and the world around us. Be flexible.

Our actions and decisions do help shape us and how we view ourselves. For me and just talking about me I have at times seen myself not as a failure but someone who continually makes mistakes. Does not matter what I do; it's always wrong. I have had plenty of people and circumstances to remind me of that.

You have to train yourself to articulate and honor your feelings and thoughts. Then you must ask yourself are your feelings true. Most times they are not accurate but a good indicator that something is going on inside you. Honor your feelings, they are important, because they will help you shape your actions to change through passion and desire.

What I wanted to share with you about actions is that sometimes doing things that don't represent your values can make it hard to look in the mirror and like what you see. That is because your internal image and what you see if the mirror are different or maybe even the same but just not what you thought you would be.

What I want to say is that your actions in life have to be consistent with your values and with your life purpose. To do so otherwise long term will result in a life that is tragic. Does it have to end in tragedy to be wasted or just a life wasted. Maybe everyone thinks your great and your perfect but how do you feel about your self and do you love and respect the person staring back at you in the mirror.

Actions / Decisions

Decisions that we make are a result of the emotional state that we are in as well as the thought process that we have developed of how things work.

Actions are an expression of faith or fear. They are an expression of our thoughts.

Actions are an expression of beliefs, emotional states and how we use our bodies.

Actions are an expression of the will or right and responsibility to choose.

To not act is also a decision.

*Actions if they become habitual or done on a regular basis like smoking will start to
Create a destiny because action sets the course.*

If new or conflicting actions are taken then the course is changed.

Actions are usually followed by waiting for the consequence of your decision. It is like planting a seed there is a time between planting and harvesting the result.

Mistakes don't necessarily ruin your life because different actions can be taken to get a different result. If your actions are in line with your internal beliefs and desires then the outward manifestation of that will come that much sooner.

Destiny

Destiny is the study of consequences. If you want to understand how you arrived at your destination or we should say your current situation you have to go all the way back to where you started and understand how you developed your thought process, how your emotional states influenced your decisions, and begin to create a new future starting where you are and not where you have been. You can create a new destiny by creating a new mission for your life, new beliefs, references for them, spiritual meaning, and powerful emotional states for success.

I have seen a lot of people in my life who should have failed. They started out with everything you could imagine against them. Maybe they lost a limb in an accident or a parent when they were young. I myself should have accomplished nothing with my life.

We can predict our own future and be the prophet of our own destiny. We have to master these skills in this book but more than that we have to reasonably predict the outcomes of our decisions and learn to properly connect where we are to the decisions we have made as adults.

The choice is yours but we have to stop the blame game. I can go back and be filled with rage and hate for so many. Honestly there are many that I don't want in my life. They pretend as if they have done nothing wrong and I wonder how many other young women have they stolen their innocence. I am a fighter and not a quitter and I won't let someone else determine my value in the end and you should not either.

Image Coaching:

Study the image matrix and understand the individual components and how the fit together to form the image that you have of yourself.

Also understand how image is used in media to shape opinion and decisions
Begin to make plans for new experiences whether it is travel or relationships that will help to broaden and even change your belief systems.

Become aware of your outlook and speech patterns especially under pressure. Ask yourself what I have to believe in order to feel this way and make this decision. Stop and ask yourself a different empowering question to cause your self to access new resources.

Become determined to become a student of outcomes and consequences and to live your life by both.

CHAPTER 5

THE BELIEFS OF THE DISTORTED SELF IMAGE

"When you change the way you look at things, the things you look at change"

Wayne Dyer

Someone once asked me how you know that the image of yourself or how you see things is distorted. I think there is two easy ways but both require a certain amount of self awareness. First I think you have to be aware of your speech. The things you say reveal a lot about what is going on inside you, both emotionally and your thought process. Second I think that you have to become aware of how you feel and how you respond when faced with different circumstances whether patterns show up in your regular routine or faced with stressful situations. Becoming aware of both will help you better determine the right questions to ask yourself.

We talked earlier about emotional states and how they affect the decision making process. In talking about belief systems we see how powerful layered belief systems and your associations are in determining your actions and reactions to situations.

No matter who you are or what your background is most of us have a distorted self image of ourselves. Why, because most of us had the influence of others as well as environment that shaped how we evaluate ourselves. None of us lived in Utopia; if you did then you have a false image of the world and your place in it. Our world is not perfect and we who make us this world are not perfect either.

No matter how strong emotionally you are or how well you were brought up, you don't know who you are or what you are capable until you face challenges. Challenges bruise us; the bruises are reminders of the battles that are here to teach us and cause growth. Like it or not we are most defined in crisis. Some see those same challenges as insurmountable events in their lives and themselves as victims. To them life is eternally unfair and hard; filled with unending pain and lack of opportunity. I did not choose the lessons in life that I wanted to learn and I don't think you did either but I can now as an adult choose my response.

There are many belief systems that empower us as well as leave us completely ineffective and impotent. Let's examine some basic beliefs of the distorted self image.

Distorted Belief #1

I NEED SOMEONE ELSE TO TELL ME WHAT TO DO

Seeking wisdom concerning a situation is not the same as seeking someone to tell you what choice to make. Our problems and challenges in our life are just that; ours. People merely can offer perspective, advice and clarity; they cannot really offer you anything else. For someone else to direct or live your life is like someone giving you directions from another car and trying to steer yours at the same time.

I know that in my life I have developed a bad habit of trying to confirm my thoughts decisions with others. There was a time though I relegated most of my life to someone else to decide. I am embarrassed to say that I did not even put gas into my own car for years. I still remember the first time I bought a cell phone or even a car. Each decision on my own was a small victory toward developing myself into a responsible adult.

Many times when faced with problems we naturally seek the advice of others. This is okay; we all need perspective and different points of view. If this is taken even half a step further into asking others for what we should do in a situation defeats the whole purpose of life's challenges. We are offered challenges because life wants us to reach our full potential. Challenges offer us a mirror into which we can see ourselves more clearly than at any other times.

There is an old saying that we you squeeze and orange what comes out of it is what it is in its nature.

When pressure is put on you how do you react? What comes out? Maybe that is what is within you.

Destiny is the study of consequences. It is and will always be our responsibility to accept the challenges of life navigate through them and evolve, shirking your responsibility to build your life will only to lead to immaturity and ruin.

Distorted Belief # 2

I HATE THE PERSON IN THE MIRROR

The mirror is a powerful tool because few of us get past the blemishes and the imperfections that we see staring back at us. The wrinkles and age spots showing through the makeup are cause for alarm as we grow older. So much of our esteem in our society is directly proportioned to our looks and ability to command superficial attention from others.

The image we see in the mirror as we grow older can become more uncomfortable. Our physical changes to due to age whether gaining weight or wrinkles is not the deeper image in which I speak. The true image of a person who has lived his or her life well or wasted it has a more lasting affect on whether we shy away from the mirror or can look back over the landscape of our life with peace; knowing it was a life well lived.

Some of us see far worse and have a distorted image so bad they we can no longer see the true reflection but only what we choose to see or one chosen for us. True definition has nothing to do with outward appearances or past experiences. A deep love of self and others can be cultivated in a healthy way so that we don't fear the reflection; we embrace it.

It's not natural to hate yourself or to hate your reflection. This is not to say that honest reflection about your life or who you are is not necessary, it is. Many times I have looked at my life and did not like what I saw. It was the condition and the decisions that I made that I hated but not me as a person. In life we have to separate ourselves from some of the mistakes we have made.

I want to talk for a minute about the effect that negative people can have on us. Negative people can over-time destroy our self image by constantly giving us negative imagery about who we are and what we are capable of. Our self image is up to us to build, by working on our belief systems, becoming more self aware of what we our potential is and finding reasons to see the beauty in us. Learn to love the person in the mirror.

Distorted Belief #3

IT NEVER WORKS FOR ME SO WHY TRY?

Defeated, I dare say most of us are disconnected from our dreams and that our lives are mostly on auto pilot just living at the line of mediocrity and far below what we are capable of. We have lost our faith, passion, and given up on our dreams. We only celebrate the lives of athletes and entertainers who can change our state of mind one hour at a time.

We look up to people in the public eye who are prettier than we are, thinner, who have money or successful careers and are more accepted and loved than us. We don't understand that though their circumstances are different, many times that are worse. They seem to live the lives we wish we had but for every report of a glamorous live there is another of a public figure whose life is a train wreck.

We have to get plugged into our lives again. We have to find someone to model the success for us that we want and be determined to live for a reason larger than our own comfort, our own conformity, and live up to our own convictions.

You can't be defined by your past failures because they can't be changed or relied on as the precedent for your future. Many of the past mistakes that you have made can be changed by changing the belief and action that caused the failure. Sometimes it's as simple as having the wrong information, making the wrong evaluation of the opportunity, and worse not making a decision at all.

Most successful people and great leaders would rather see you do something and make a mistake than do nothing at all. Movement is a requirement of success. The most successful people can gather information and have found a way to assess the meaning of that information and interpret the risk associated with it. We have to learn to lead, manage, and serve our futures in this way.

Failure is actually a good thing. Failure is just a way of doing things that did not work. It's a system of doing things that produced a different result than the one you wanted. Most belief that failure is essential to long term success because is makes you change and find a way to get the results you want.

So why do so many people not try when success is possible for anyone doing almost anything. I think most people give up not do to a lack of will power but knowing what to do when mistakes are made. I believe that many times that I have given up; I would not have it someone would have shown be a better way or helped me with the next step. Let me add that to make it one you have to have a team concept. Second you need mentors who can help you along the way. Too many times we simply choose critics and not people who can add real value to our journey.

"Your surroundings, home, personal care, pets, clothing & body are all reflections of how you see and express yourself. Do these reflect your true self"?

Christiane Northrup, M.D.

Image Coaching:

Decide not to be driven by a negative self image or yourself or life and develop a new belief system that can propel you into a successful and happy future.

Begin to make decisions for yourself researching information and making predictions based on past results that reasonably predict outcomes in the future.

Begin to speak to the person in the mirror with strength and with love. Learn to speak the language of forgiveness and grace to yourself and others. Be slow to speak and quick to listen.

CHAPTER 6

THE HABITS OF A DISTORTED SELF IMAGE

"Never compare your inside with somebody else outside."

Hugh Macleod

In the previous chapter we looked at some of the beliefs of a distorted self image. There are many others but one thing they have in common is that none of them empower the individual. Why don't you take some time and in your journal and ask yourself what you believe about yourself that defines your self-image both for good and bad. What do you really see, when you see yourself?

Great lives are built over time. Many people who rise quickly fall just as fast. So it could be said that the little decisions we make everyday and how we calculate the risks and consequence of our decisions is really where the battle is won.

Let's talk about some of the habits in our lives that cause us to fail and have a defeated self image.

Habit #1

FOCUS ON THE PROBLEM RATHER THAN THE SOLUTION

Einstein once said that if you want to solve a problem you have to think at a higher level than what caused the problem. Enough said. Focus on the solution and not the problem. If you want to be rich solve your problems and then solve them for someone else.

Focus allows us to put all of our mental energy into the object that we are focusing on. Living the Max Life systems teaches that you experience is changed largely by what you focus on. So if you focus on the problem or the negative in any situation you only experience more of the negative caused by the situation or obstacle.

If you choose to focus on the positive in any situation you give yourself an opportunity to experience something different. If you choose to expend your energy looking for the solution to a problem rather than focusing on what you cant do or what was done wrong you can change the circumstance. Focus on the solution.

Habit #2

UNFORGIVENESS AND DWELL IN THE PAST

I want to share just two words with you. Forgive and release. Not forgiving someone else or yourself keeps crippling memories rotating like driving 55 on a flat tire. Trust me sooner or later your on the rim and going no where fast.

People with distorted images of themselves don't let go of past hurts. One of the main reasons is that to hold onto grudges and negative emotions create certainty in that situation. It may be painful but it is less painful to hold onto it than it is to let it go.

In our society we are big on punishment; not the kind of in the moment calculated punishment but long drawn out I am going to make you suffer punishment. The distorted part really comes in when we think that we don't deserve the best in life, family, relationships, jobs, etc. We don't learn to forgive others nor ourselves. When you are not willing to let go you are literally carrying around the weight of that issue or problem much like swimming with an anvil.

I think the worst thing about un-forgiveness is the person who won't let go suffers the most.

Habit #3

BEING CRITICAL OF EVERYONE INCLUDING YOURSELF

This person is not the life of the party so to speak, they are the one that always sees fault and lives in the land of their own judgment. Two words: who cares? Don't allow critics in your life but do allow people to critique you and your work who have only your best interest at heart. How do you know the difference; one only offers criticism while the other seeks ways to make improvements and add value.

How does this change the image? Over time is like rubbing dirt on an already dirty mirror. After a while no matter how hard you look, you can no longer see the original image. Better we live with a little dirt than looking into a dirty mirror, no matter how clean we really are, it's the dirt that we see.

Habit #4

PEOPLE WITH DISTORTED IMAGES DON'T SET GOALS

Who would buy a car without a steering wheel? Who would buy a boat, start the engine and just let it go. It will be lost at sea, run into another ship or wash up on a beach a wreck. Live your life without a reason, without goals and a way to evaluate your life; you are living without a direction; any direction or outcome will do.

Low achievers don't set goals and don't work toward anything. They wallow in self pity because they don't have the circumstances that they want and they dislike themselves too much to believe they disserve better. Remember, you were created in an image and that image has no limitations.

Setting goals is the result of an image that beliefs that you can achieve the object of your desire or need. Not setting goals is from a belief that you can't and you prefer the current ever growing level of pain rather than choosing the fight for your future and set goals to achieve it.

If you have watched *Batman Begins* or the *Dark Knight* there is a story in the movie of why he selects the bat as a symbol and part of his character. The bat was his fear that he had to overcome and represented the fear of many others. It was the image of the bat that made him more than he could be on his own. The strong image and the fear it produced made him something larger than life that could not be diminished, ignored or destroyed.

Habit #5

CREATE STATES OF DEPRESSION AND SICKNESS

There are some who are clinically depressed but most of us are not. We live in states of mind that we create for ourselves both good and bad. We develop a belief system, give ourselves plenty of references why it is right or wrong and don't evaluate whether or not it's working for us. For those who have clinical depression, they should seek immediate evaluation and help. Clinical depression may be based on a chemical imbalance in the brain that needs to be corrected.

Ask yourself what you have to belief about negative feelings you are experiencing in order to feel them for an extended period of time. Change the question to allow a positive outcome.

Go back and study emotional states and do these three things:

Write and speak aloud positive affirmations daily to reprogram your mind. Don't allow negative thoughts to stick. Wrestle with them by learning the discipline of controlling your inner thoughts. Learn to coach yourself and participate in the inner dialogue in a positive way. In doing so this is not mere affirmation but also critique and correction of thoughts and behavior.

Journal and become more self aware and spend time understanding your belief system by articulating your feelings. Through a series of questions change your beliefs and look for references to convince yourself that they are true. We have talked earlier about the power of questions. Questions are a key component to shaping beliefs as well as changing them. We ask questions to get answers and form opinions. We can ask questions to empower or that destroy. Ask your self why are you so stupid and you will get answers and anchor that belief. Ask your self how can you perform better and achieve better results and you will get that answer as well.

Create a positive supporting physiology but meditating, deep breathing, proper posture, eating right, getting proper amounts of sleep, and create a special physical response that puts you in a peak emotional state. Look at great athletes whenever he makes a great shot, there is one athlete when he makes that shot expresses it with his full emotion and does a move with a closed fist that anchors his emotional state.

Habit #6

MAKE EXCUSES

Rather than face the truth it's easier for us to make excuses of life all together. If you don't find the circumstance you want go find it somewhere else or create it. Face life with accepting the facts and the truth of the matter. Let your words be plain and simple when it comes to the truth.

Making excuses further distorts the image because you wont allow yourself to see things they way they really are. Don't make excuses for yourselves of others. While making proper evaluations of circumstances, people and actions, remember that people can be thought of separately from their mistakes. If we are our mistakes and we can't change, then where is the hope of doing it right. We are not our mistakes and we are not slave to our past wrong decisions. Learn from them and embrace the possibilities of making better decisions to create a better future.

Habit #7

PROCRASTINATE

One of the most crippling things in life is not making decisions or delaying acting on the ones you have made. Not living up to the commitments we make to ourselves and others insures a life of failure and disappointment. Redo your things to do list based on outcomes, some of the things you have committed to is just busy work and has no meaning. Articulate the 1-3 things that you can truly focus on, set goals and priorities, forget the past and get back to work.

Why do we procrastinate? Partially procrastination is a learned behavior. Some of have learned to procrastinate because our parents or others have modeled that behavior for us by making endless excuses and putting things off.

Also we procrastinate because we usually don't do a good job of calculating risk and reward. We look for the place where we can put the least effort and the greatest gain. The challenge with is that risk and reward are proportionate. If we don't act on making decision and getting things done we can feel like we can still get something that we may not have earned.

Winners don't think that way. People who achieve great things learn to evaluate the risk of doing something and the reward in doing it. If the risk of doing it makes sense commensurate to the reward they don't delay in making decisions and doing it.

Also the last main reason why we procrastinate is simply a matter of pain and pleasure. Many times doing causes discomfort and so rather than feel the discomfort we put it off until not doing it is more painful than doing it. Many people don't quit smoking until sickness, disease, or other problems manifest themselves prompting action. Even then some still do not act. Apathy should be treated as a disease that can be cured but left unattended will destroy the host.

Don't get in the habit of procrastination. Become a person of strong self image and a decisive person of action. I do because I can.

Image Coaching:

Change your life focus to something that is larger than the activity or even the image that gives your purpose.

Make your new focus large enough that your image of yourself must change to achieve it

Be determined to change your beliefs, your character before trying to change your actions and circumstances.

Don't conform; chart a new and exciting path for your life.

CHAPTER 7

BECOME THE VOICE

*"Your grief for what you've lost lifts a mirror up
to where you're bravely working"*
Mevlana Rumi (1207 - 1273)

Vividly I remember growing up that there were many voices speaking to me about who I was, what my role was and of my worth. I had a father who was an abusive alcoholic whose voice could be heard through the yelling and the physical beatings. He was telling me that I did not matter and was not loved. That I was different but not special; I was to be strong like a man, be abused and treated unfairly my whole life.

My life was contradictory as my father when sober would supply for us. He would take us to the best restaurants and make sure we were clothed well. The coin had two sides as the other side made us perform at the dinner table like circus animals. Though he clothed me, the impact I remember the most was a young girl in braw and panties thrown out of the house while it was snowing in New York. I was a young teenager at that age. I remember I had to hide behind the garbage to stay warm. My mom brought me out some food; I remember how cold it was and how embarrassed I was to be outside unclothed. I have felt exposed like that so many times in my life.

There was also a passive mother who spoke through her examples of surviving the beatings and over the years living down to what my father thought of her. A beautiful professional woman over time has become bitter and passive-dependant. I wanted so desperately my mother's love and protection. I ended up protecting her one day as my father was beating her he pulled out a machete and vowed to kill her. I stepped between them that day and told my father to kill me instead. My mother left at my request and never returned to check on me, never called, never wrote, never. Much time had past before I saw my mom again and to my surprise her leaving and having her life spared it had become my fault why she had lost her marriage to this abusive man. What was the voice telling me; once again that it was my fault. This particular voice would echo for another 30 plus years before it could be confronted and silenced.

Relatives who molested me spoke to me that I was worth nothing, an object that was there to satisfy their lustful gratifications but of no worth on my own. One that I trusted the most would ask me for favors for money. Innocent at first but I became his favorite because of our secrets. Too many women have heard that voice; it's a seductive and sometimes mean voice that pierces the soul crying out for some real love and affection. It's a cheap promise never fulfilled through even cheaper thrills on our behalf.

I remember small things like sleeping 15 to a 3 bedroom house wearing hand me downs. At times we could have been savages running through our quiet farm. I have so many good memories with my cousins, my dog boogy and my little chickens who ate the corn that I spread all over me and the ground as I was lost in watching clouds in endless formations.

I want to tell you about my dog boogy. He was a small mixed breed but very smart. My dog loved ice cream so every time we would be home and heard the ice cream truck coming I told boogy to stop the truck while I went to go and get money. I ran as fast as I could and so did boogy. He ran down the hill that our house sat on and ran into the middle of that dirt road and sat. The ice cream man would look for him because this was our normal routine. I returned with a kings ransom for Boogy's and my favorite flavor; coconut ice cream. I ate mine with one hand and held his so he could eat it.

My chickens were my friends as well. I loved to lie in the grass and let the little chickens eat the corn that I spread all over myself. My father always whistled and yelled for me as I spent hours with my animal friends. They did not talk much but they were always gracious enough to listen.

I miss my mountains for they spoke to me as well. In their grandeur I was safe from the wrath of my father. The still air was always interrupted by whistling; not for dogs, this familiar call was for me.

I remember one time becoming so angry after another incident. I had no one to talk to no one to understand what I was going through. I remember lying down in a pile of ants and letting them bite me. I was swollen with bites from head to toe and had to be taken to the emergency room that night. I learned that physical pain was easier to take and could be a much needed distraction from emotional pain. I remember jumping out of trees, poles, fences, cutting myself and many self destructive things to cause temporary pain. It was wrong but it reminded me that I was alive and provided an escape from my harsh reality.

I learned over the years as my voice grew louder that it was not my voice at all but a clamoring of many voices of both positive and negative that had shaped by experience and beliefs. I was speaking this same death that was spoken into me and if I was to change and speak forth the love that I had known from God then I would have to become the voice that spoke in my life.

Becoming the Voice

Let's talk about the voice and what it is. The voice in our life is first the internal language that we speak to ourselves. It is also the voice of others who have shaped how we feel and what we believe about ourselves. It's the voice telling us that we can't or that we are fat, dumb, stupid, and ugly or an array of things.

This internal language as we have discussed earlier is one of the three contributing factors of our emotional state. Simply what we say to ourselves is our internal language. What we say to ourselves about our relationships, circumstances, hopes, dreams and the possibilities of our lives.

The other part of our voice is what we say to others. Many times what I spoke to others was really my past speaking through me. The traditions of our parents were passed down; many times because they thought it was the right thing to teach us because it was how they were taught. I have learned that we have to reject the religion (world view) of our fathers and mothers and choose our own values and path. I did not say reject the God of our fathers or mothers but reject some of the traditions. As adults our path must be our own and some of what we were taught stifles our growth and development. Even religion or a true relationship with God is a constant unfolding revelation. What parent does not want more for his child that what he has or has become?

All that I was taught about myself and the world around me stifled me because it was mostly negative. What I was taught about others of other ethnicity and cultures were my parents hang ups. We must learn to challenge our beliefs and renew our minds to new possibilities. From these new believes we must learn to speak to ourselves first and then to others.

Over time my internal dialogue has changed. I remember for years I did not look in the mirror because of the person who stared back at me. My self concept was shaped by what was said to me and the language of the treatment. As I grew I found myself finding the strength to believe that I was okay and later that I was actually beautiful.

I did not have to succumb to the anger and hatred of my father. Though I was called a boy for many years I could believe that I could be feminine. I could be a woman. It has taken a long time and through much fear and trepidation I have slowly become the voice speaking to myself and others.

Ask yourself if you consciously paid attention to what you said every day. Would you speak life or death to yourself and others; words of faith or fear? Become the voice in your life. You are the greatest prophet of your future as well as the future of many others.

Image Coaching:

Start journaling today if you don't already journal. Nothing will help you develop an empowering internal voice as fast as journaling because it gives you a safe avenue of expression.

Start learning to tell people how you really feel. Be respectful and don't do it to hurt people but do it to join the conversation of your life. Don't let anyone control your voice, its time to be heard and appreciated.

Start new hobbies and activities that are uniquely you. Don't worry if no one else want to participate; this should be an expression of your internal voice, not someone else.

Remember fear is not a part of your new life. You must move toward truth, power and love and away from fear, lies, and weakness.

CHAPTER 8

LIFE ON PURPOSE

*"We cannot see our reflection in running water.
It is only in still water that we can see"*
Taoist Proverb

In 2005 I grew restless of the life that I had come to live over the years. What I had not realized is that I had always lived a small part of my dreams of helping people. For over 12 years I have worked in the Central Florida community helping people in various jobs and positions. I knew that I wanted to do something more; something different. What was this new voice that spoke to me?

Prior to starting the foundation I had done a lot of community work through the Catholic Church at one time as well as serving other families at Christmas. There was a new direction stirring inside me that called for expression. A friend told me in a conversation that I should go and volunteer for the Central Florida Coalition for the Homeless. I had spoken to him about wanting to get involved in the community and reaching out to families in need.

I started out with one family in 2005 sponsoring them for Christmas. There was a mother, father and two children both boys. This was my first family that I sponsored for Christmas. I met them with my family at the Coalition outside. We greeted each other warmly on this cold December morning. My son talked to their sons as my husband, daughter and I spoke to the parents. I remember special moments in this encounter that I would never forget.

The mother upon receiving a new jacket at a present began to cry as she said that she had never gotten a new jacket her entire life. Each gift brought out noises of excitement that at times were uncontrollable and could only be described by a warmed heart. There were many tears and hugs that day; but more was to come.

The next day a friend of mine and I loaded them up and drove them to Disney World. We gave them the tickets, some money, and digital cameras to remember the occasion. It was two days that would not soon be forgotten.

Some time later we found out that the mother had been arrested for drugs and prostitution. The two boys and father were living in the woods away from the confines of the shelter. I saw the father and boys around town passing by on buses or coming out of the woods. We had brief encounters but I remember most of all that they eyes of those two boys lit up each time they saw me as if it were still Christmas.

The next Christmas we sponsored 5 families, the year after that 10, then 15 and in 2007 we sponsored 37 families within the WRCC (a division of the Coalition for the Homeless). The Christmas Wish has grown every year but we make sure to spend personal time with each and every family. It's never been our mission to drop off gifts but to spend time and share the Christmas spirit in love.

In life too many times and for too long we live life on auto pilot. Life for many is wrapped up in their circumstances and definitions placed on them by others.

In 2007 WP Foundation started teaching a personal development seminar called *Living the Max Life*. I also teach a Self Image seminar called Hidden Potential that is part of the Max Life curriculum. Max Life is a complete program for success that breaks life down into individually mastering 5 maxims. Spirituality, Emotional and Mental health, Physical health, Financial Health, and Life Mastery are the 5 maxims. The purpose of the program is to give people the tools to help them to live their life on purpose and with purpose.

We live life with purpose when we can articulate our hopes, dreams and pursue them within our own defined values and truths. What have you defined as your purpose? When you work on changing your self image to one that is powerful and full of life then your purpose is revealed along with it. Meaning is essential to seeing yourself the way you were created. We have to choose values and purposes for our gifts and talents that are larger than us and not for the pursuit of material gain and personal greed. Our purpose must be connected to living a life of service and leaving a footprint on this planet that leaves an impression that leaves this planet better than when you found it.

Dare to see you empowered to make a difference, develop a strategy and create powerful emotional states to support it. Take massive action and accomplish small goals along the way of creating a grand vision for your life.

Image Coaching:

If you are reading this book start a new journey in a new direction today. Let this become the beginning of self improvement and investment.

Use the knowledge you have acquired and continue to study; see learning as a life long pursuit.

In order to get something you have never gotten, do something you have never done.

Make the change, change the image, and change your life.

CHAPTER 9

NEW IMAGE NEW LIFE

"Just remember when looking in the mirror, it is always looking back at you...the reflections seen are only ever as kind or as ill as your own projections."

Morrigan

A new image of yourself and the world around you will literally change your life. I know my life has changed drastically as I have worked hard to change the way I see myself, others, and the world around me.

Our world view is our paradigm; it's our mental map of the world. It tells us how the world works and how to navigate through the challenges. If your map is wrong or does not change with the changing terrain then you will be sure about where you think you are until it dawns on you that you're lost.

My map of the world was built on fear and mistrust; opportunities that were not coming as I watched more blessed people than I get what they wanted out of life. In this world there really are three things that we want to modify or change. The first is how we feel. I have never met anyone who did not want to feel better or feel something different.

Changing our behavior is another thing that we want to change. I hate telling this story but growing up the way that I did, fear dominated my life. I was afraid of bad weather, the dark, men, and being on my own. My family knew my fears and accepted them; actually they and many others enabled my fears. One thing I will share with you is that I was so afraid of the dark that I would turn off the light in the bathroom and run as fast as I could and jump into bed. I had to sleep with the covers over me and no matter what I could not leave my feet exposed as I was afraid that someone would grab them.

I know this is silly but you would be surprised what people do when no one is looking. What about the person smoking or being promiscuous to be accepted or the women prostituting herself for another hit of drugs to mask the pain of her daily existence. We want to change our behavior and live a more productive life. A life that is more in line with what our insides says that we are or the lifestyle we dreamed of as kids.

The third major thing that we want to change is the outcomes or the results we achieve. I know that in my life I have had many victories and many battles that were lost along the way. I think it is impossible to win all the time or even be perfect, but have you ever entered a season in your life where nothing you tried went right? It's very difficult to live with your dreams differed.

The question really does become how do I feel something different than what I have felt before, how can I change my behavior, and how can I achieve the outcomes that I really want with my life. At this point I hope you have begun the tough work of changing your self image for a more empowering life but at the end of the day I want something different than the failure and rejection that I have known.

Step 1

Desire

I think desire is the first step to achieve anything. You have to have strong desire and a vision or dream that is not abstract but is clear and concise. Take more time out by yourself and think about the life you want to live and why. Think about it would feel to achieve it and how you would want others to feel about you if you did.

Write down this dream, vision or thing that you desire. Read it daily and let your whole being be infected by the desire to achieve it. Believe that it is possible and remind yourself of this knew person that you see in the mirror of your circumstances.

Step 2

Strategy

You have to articulate something and make it tangible by developing a plan to get it. I am always amazed at how much energy people will put into something that they want but they have no strategy to get it or achieve it.

If you need help find someone who has achieved the result your looking for, find out how they did it and model their behavior and beliefs. Yes, ask them what they believed or told themselves in the process of achieving it.

Step 3

Education

I think you have to get the facts. Too many times we start projects and undertake great ideas without getting the facts of what it will take to do it.

Also once you do achieve it make sure you have the education or right questions asked and answered to maintain it. Don't set yourself up for failure. Learn everything you can about the thing that you want to achieve.

Education is a life long pursuit. I hope when you put down this book that you will pick up as many others as you can and continue your journey of knowledge, wisdom, and understanding.

Step 4

Meditate

Even before you start actually working on your goal, I believe that you should meditate and focus on what you are about to go after. See yourself connected to it, the conditions you need to achieve it and don't allow yourself or anyone else to put doubt into your mind.

Step 5

Create Massive Action

ACT! The first step and the last step are the hardest but the faster you move toward your goal and with each movement toward it EVERYDAY you will get closer and closer to achieving it.

You create massive action by focus. Make this one of the top priorities of your life that you work on everyday. Also create affirmations to support your self mentally and form good habits that are in line with achieving the goal and not a distraction from it.

Your actions have to be in line with what you want. If you want to stop overeating stop hanging out with friends that you always eat with; making eating the center of your social life will guarantee that you don't modify your behavior or get different results.

You have to start being around someone who can model for you the outcomes that you want to achieve.

If you want to loose weight get with someone who has. Learn from them on what their plan was, what they do, what they think when they face temptation.

Step 6

Journal / Evaluate

I believe one of the most powerful tools for achieving a life of success is journaling. I write about it and teach it all the time. Journaling is like putting up sign posts along the way that help you stay focused and keep track of where you are.

Journaling also gives voice to your feelings and challenges along the way. Being able to get it out of your head and onto paper allows you to go back and look at it and balance your feelings with reasoning. This will help you make critical adjustments when you stray off course.

Step 7

Have Fun

Have fun. Why put energy into the creation of something if it is not fun along the way or fun when you get it. Loving life is a strong motivator and having fun keeps you young and vibrant.

You should ask yourself on the fun meter what would I rate my experiences from 1-10. Then ask yourself if it is not a 10 then what could I do to make it a 10. Creating an atmosphere where you and others are going to have fun and enjoy the experience should be built into everything you do.

Predetermining how you want to feel is important. Would you get married without associating a feeling with it? No you would not. We buy into things, commit, and even purchase things based on what experience we hope to have. We develop a perceived value.

The problem is that you don't associate actions and consequences with the feelings you experienced. That is why some people don't learn from the mistakes that they make. So predetermine how you want to feel and make sure that your decisions and outcomes line up to create the experience and feelings you want.

I have shared with you the power of a healthy self image and the pain of one that is defined by another and distorted. I encourage you today to take responsibility for the condition of your life, define the things you want, write it, read it, and take action on it. You become the voice that defines your image and importance in the world and go out there and be great. Living the Max life is just that; living a divine inspired life of service in which you have articulated and worked hard to create the outcomes that you desired and were created with the ability to do.

Create a new image, put references in place to create a new belief system. Engage your internal language to support your new image and direction and use your physiology in a more powerful way. Create a new image and experience a new life on your own terms.

Image Coaching:

When creating a new image allow it to be just that; a new image. If you must look back, look through the eyes of triumph. Remember not so much the defeats unless you can learn from them but remember the times that you overcame obstacles and hardships.

Develop a life of self discipline focused on learning and evolving into a larger image than your past.

Become a life long learner and begin to trust again as you allow people to critique you and offer insight and not criticism.

Guard your heart but leave room for love and experiencing the finer things in life.

Never loose hope!

Never give up!

Always be a tree of encouragement, giving shade for those to have a place to retreat.

Wanda Perez is a speaker, personal development coach and a certified trainer with the Living the Max Life System. For further information, books, free resources and event listing please go to www.livingthemaxlife.com and click on Hidden Potential.

This has been a Creative Media Concepts published work to help you improve every area of your life and develop a new self image. If you would like to contact Ayub Fleming or Wanda Perez please go to www.info@livingthemaxlife.com.

For more information on the WP Foundation and what we are doing in the community and how you can partner with us, go to www.worldpromise-foundation.com.

www.ingramcontent.com/pod-product-compliance
Lightning Source LLC
Chambersburg PA
CBHW071637050426
42443CB00026B/640